Wooden Spoon
The children's charity of rugby

RUGBYWORLD
Yearbook 2015

Editor
Ian Robertson

Photographs
Getty Images

Published in the UK in 2014 by
Lennard Publishing, an imprint of
Lennard Associates Ltd,
Mackerye End,
Harpenden, Herts AL5 5DR
email: orders@lennardqap.co.uk

Distributed by G2 Entertainment
c/o Orca Book Services
160 Eastern Avenue, Milton Park
Abingdon, OX14 4SB

ISBN: 978-1-85291-157-7

Production editor: Chris Marshall
Text and cover design: Paul Cooper

Caricature of Steve Borthwick on page 33 by John Ireland

The publishers would like to thank Getty Images for providing most of the photographs for
this book. The publishers would also like to thank AIG, Fotosport UK, Fotosport Italy, Inpho
Photography, IRB, Chris Thau and Wooden Spoon for additional material.

Printed and bound in Italy
by L.E.G.O. S.p.A

Contents

Financial institutions   Energy   Infrastructure, mining and commodities

Aberdeen
Simply asset management.

Aberdeen Asset
Management is proud
to support Wooden
Spoon, the children's
charity of rugby.

FOREWORD

by HRH THE PRINCESS ROYAL

BUCKINGHAM PALACE

HRH The Princess Royal,
Royal Patron of Wooden Spoon.

Since its origins in 1983 Wooden Spoon has enhanced the lives of over one million children and young people in need across the British Isles. Now in its 31st year, Wooden Spoon has donated over £22 million and supported over 650 projects across the UK including specialist schools and other charities and community projects that give support, treatment or respite care to children with disabling or life-limiting medical conditions or who are living in areas of severe social deprivation.

The past year represents a consecutive period of growth for Wooden Spoon with over £1.8 million committed to support children and young people in need. Another most welcome development is the growth of Wooden Spoon into Ireland where the charity is already raising local funds for local projects.

Wooden Spoon is inspired and motivated by its rugby heritage and the support of its volunteers and the rugby community. The Rugby World Cup in England and Wales in 2015 provides the platform for Wooden Spoon to raise additional funds, to support more children and young people in need, and extend the profile of the charity across the international rugby community.

As Patron of Wooden Spoon I wish everyone involved with fundraising through this milestone year great success and I would like to thank you for your interest and enthusiasm. This is a unique and vibrant charity that has achieved much, but can and will achieve a lot more with your support both now and in the future.

Anne

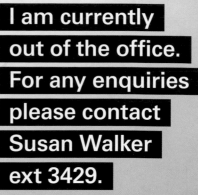

I am currently out of the office. For any enquiries please contact Susan Walker ext 3429.

Crunch, swish, crunch, swish, that's the soundtrack of an uncomplicated life. It's a place that has the freshest of air, the whitest of snow and bluest of blue sky. It's an experience that makes it feel great to be alive. We understand that the time you spend away from the office is just as important as the time you spend at it and that it's all connected. And it's only when we look at all the different aspects of your life together, that we are able to see your personal economy. Something that's unique to you and constantly changing. So at HSBC Premier we focus on providing personal support, for your personal economy.

Find out more at hsbcpremier.com/personaleconomy

HSBC Premier is subject to financial eligibility criteria.

Proud supporter of the Wooden Spoon.

Wooden Spoon
The children's charity of rugby

Wooden Spoon is a charity dedicated to supporting children and young people who are disadvantaged physically, mentally or socially.

We support a diverse range of projects and not just one particular need, illness or disability. Our work has benefited over 1 million children and so far we have granted over £22 million to projects such as sensory rooms, respite and medical centres and specialist playgrounds across the UK.

Please help us to continue our work and visit woodenspoon.com

Wooden Spoon, 115 - 117 Fleet Road, Fleet, Hampshire, GU51 3PD, Charity Registration No 326691 (England & Wales) and SC039247 (Scotland)

Wooden Spoon
The children's charity of rugby

WHO WE ARE

Wooden Spoon is a grant making charity founded in 1983. Since then we have been committed to helping improve the lives of disabled and disadvantaged children.

We are one of the largest UK funders of respite and medical treatment centres, sensory rooms, specialist playgrounds, sports activity areas, and community-based programmes and have so far granted over £22 million to these fantastic projects.

Inspired and motivated by our rugby heritage and by working together with the rugby community, with the support of its top sporting heroes, we have been able to help over 1 million children and fund over 650 projects.

In 2011 Wooden Spoon became the first charity to receive the Spirit of Rugby Award from the International Rugby Board and in November 2013 became the official charity partner of the Rugby League World Cup. We are also honoured to have HRH The Princess Royal as our Patron.

THE STORY BEHIND WOODEN SPOON

A wonderful legacy emerged in 1983 after five England rugby supporters went to Dublin to watch England in the final game of the Five Nations Championship against the Irish. The game was lost 25-15 and England finished last in the table with just a single point gained from their draw against Wales.

After the match, in a Dublin bar surrounded by celebrating Ireland supporters, the five England supporters sought some consolation only for three of their Irish friends to present them with a wooden spoon, wrapped in an Irish scarf on a silver platter as a memento of England's dismal season.

Accepting the gift with good humour and grace, the England fans resolved to hold a golf match to see who would have the honour of keeping the wooden spoon. Just a few months later the golf match was held and in the course of an entertaining day an astonishing sum of £8,450 was raised. The money was used to provide a new minibus for a local special needs school, Park School. This was to be the of first many Wooden Spoon charitable projects that has grown to over 600 in the years since.

From defeat on the rugby field, and a tongue-in-cheek consolation prize, the Wooden Spoon charity was born.

OUR ROYAL PATRON

Our Royal Patron is HRH The Princess Royal who gives generously of her time.

OUR RUGBY PATRONS

The IRFU, RFU, WRU, SRU, RFL all support us in our charitable work.

SPORTING PARTNERS

We work closely with a variety of clubs, league associations and governing bodies who help us achieve our vision of improving young lives though the power of rugby.

WOODEN SPOON PROJECTS

As a grant making charity Wooden Spoon provides funding to organisations such as specialist schools, other charities and community projects that provide support, treatment or respite care for children with disabling or life-limiting medical conditions or living in areas of severe social deprivation. With the money raised by Wooden Spoon, some incredible things have been achieved across the UK. We are so proud of all the worthy causes that we help fund, and here are just a few of these projects we have funded this year alone.

MARY HARE SCHOOL FOR DEAF CHILDREN

Mary Hare School for Deaf Children in Newbury benefited from a grant of £39,200 to fully refurbish the mathematics department, the first upgrade of the maths area of the school in over 25 years. The refurbishment included the installation of new infra-red technology, allowing teachers to communicate with pupils through the school's Group Hearing Aid to become "wireless". The refurbishment also included the installation of two disabled access stair-lifts which will allow pupils with restricted mobility to move around the school's maths teaching area more easily.

We are truly grateful for Wooden Spoon's generous support for our project to "refurbish the teaching areas in the school as well as making it more accessible for those pupils who have mobility difficulties".

- Tony Shaw, CEO & Principal Mary Hare School for Deaf Children

GAME ON GLASGOW

Game on Glasgow engages with young people who are not in employment, education or training through rugby, by focusing their energies and instilling the rugby values of discipline, teamwork and respect. Combining sporting activity with specialist training and vital work experience, helping young people get into jobs and education. This programme aims to build the confidence, self belief and personal skills among the young people taking part.

Reece was excluded from school at the age of 14. His behaviour and lack of motivation prevented him from engaging with education and also his peers. With the help of the Game On Programme he became more confident and motivated, going on to complete Stage 3 Employability Fund training, and has now successfully gained part time employment with Subway.

"I have learnt more skills and gained knowledge about rugby which I have really enjoyed, and hope to keep playing in the future".

- Reece, 17

NORTHERN IRELAND CANCER FUND FOR CHILDREN

Northern Ireland Cancer Fund for Children received a £54,000 donation for a The Wooden Spoon Playroom as part of their new respite centre in County Down, Newcastle. The creation of the new playroom provides hours of fun for children going through a very difficult time, offering a happy distraction and helping to make their stay at the centre more enjoyable.

"We can't thank Wooden Spoon enough for this marvellous donation. It's the gift that will just keep on giving for families facing the devastation of cancer".

- Gillian Creevy, Cancer Fund for Children CEO

RIVERSIDE RDA

Riverside RDA in Yorkshire received £25,000 for The Wooden Spoon Stable Block and was opened by the HRH The Princess Royal. The new stable block is big enough to accommodate all the ponies and provide an area where the disabled youngsters can work with the horses in a safe and secure environment. They can groom the ponies and help muck out the stables in addition to having their riding lesson. The new classroom in the Stable Block provides the opportunity for the riders to learn more about horses, including colours, breeds, points of the horse and feeding. They can also work towards their RDA Grades and an ASDAN qualification. Princess Anne is a patron of both Riding for Disabled (RDA) and Wooden Spoon, making this project opening for the Yorkshire region extra special.

"It's incredible to see how much children benefit from being with horses. We have children with Asperger's and autism who quieten and calm down the moment they sit on a pony. It's wonderful, and we're very, very lucky to have got this donation".

- Moira Wragg, Riverside's chief instructor

WITCHFORD VILLAGE COLLEGE

Witchford Village College in Cambridgeshire received £4,865 towards the creation of The Wooden Spoon Sensory Garden. The pupils at the College suffer from a wide range of disabilities including Autism, Asperger's Syndrome and ADHD, while others are classified as suffering from behavioural and emotional difficulties, sometimes as a result of domestic/parental abuse.

The new garden will provide a number of benefits to the pupils such as helping with social awareness and teamwork, offer a safe space for vulnerable and at-risk pupils, encourage outdoor learning and practical activities and help pupils connect with their senses.

"I have learnt so much about plants and how to look after them. I water the garden all the time and it helps me calm down if I get angry".

- Kieran, Year 10 Student.

THE 1974 BRITISH AND IRISH LIONS 40TH ANNIVERSARY REUNION!

The British and Irish Lions of 1974 sat on their bus outside Loftus Versfeld Stadium, belting out Flower of Scotland. To a man the future Invincibles joined impassioned chorus, led by lock Gordon Brown. The nonplussed Springboks filed past into the ground: Fergus Slattery knew the Lions were headed for victory. If the controversial '99' call warned South Africa the visitors would truck no backward step, that impromptu rendition declared a pride of Lions singing off the same hymn sheet.

"Gordon stood up at the front of the bus, started singing, sat back down and everyone joined in," recounted Ireland's stellar flank-forward Fergus Slattery.
"Just as Gordon got the orchestra into gear if you like, the South Africa team bus pulled up and all their players got off. All they could see was all the Lions sat still on the bus, just singing. They all walked past us and into the ground, and you could see them looking back, hearing us and wondering what was going on. Flower of Scotland was our tour song, it was our national anthem if you want to call it that: it was a unifying force. Remember all the squad was on the bus, not just those involved in the match. It was pure coincidence they pulled up at the same time, it wasn't a piece of show business or anything – but it definitely unnerved them."

The Lions triumphed 28-9 on June 22, 1974 in Pretoria, eventually claiming a 3-0 series victory. Willie John McBride's men drew the fourth Test 13-13, but returned home unbeaten. Some 40 years on those exploits remain chiselled into the core of rugby's very annals. Wooden Spoon Ulster branch chairman Peter Wood led the duo in coordinating 22 of the 1974 touring squad meeting up in Ireland in June for a series of 40th anniversary reunion events.

"They were a most remarkable group of guys and in our own way we made a little bit of history, and that's something we all treasure," said tour skipper McBride.
"I went on five tours and there was never a bond quite like this tour, I don't know why but they were just that sort of people. And we were never beaten, so those were all things that pulled us together. I'll never forget one bus journey back to the Culloden Hotel in Belfast where we were staying. We'd had a barbecue and on the bus back we were all singing all the old songs again, just like we had on the tour: it just gelled straight away again, it was unbelievable. These guys have come through life with great humility. Peter Wood carried out a tremendous amount of work himself, and he deserves a huge amount of credit for bringing things together."

McBride, Gareth Edwards, Andy Irvine, JPR and JJ Williams and Phil Bennett officially opened a new Wooden Spoon-backed children's playroom at the Daisy Lodge in Newcastle, County Down, supported by the Northern Ireland Cancer Fund for Children. Wooden Spoon sponsors Flybe then renamed one of their fleet The Invincibles in the squad's honour, before gala dinners at Belfast's Hastings Culloden Hotel and Dublin's Ballsbridge Hotel.

Slattery said the latest gatherings could be the last official reunion, revealing the pride and humility still accompanying an achievement "undiminished" by the intervening years.

"I think this probably will be the last reunion of its ilk to be honest," conceded Slattery.
"Willie John McBride, who was at the older end of that generation, I think he might keep his powder dry rather than promote 50th anniversary reunions! In '74 I was up training at the club the week we got back, and we had the Ireland centenary, so we had Test matches three weeks after we came home. So you may have been great on the Lions tour but it was over straight away. No one spent any time dwelling on it. And I think as much as everyone involved remains hugely proud of those times, if you asked them, they would still view it the same way."

Wooden Spoon's Ulster committee chairman Wood hailed the summer reunions as the region's top highlight to date. "The 1974 Lions Reunion was undoubtedly our highlight of 2014 and indeed any other year," he said. "Wooden Spoon Ulster would like to thank Willie John McBride and Syd Millar for allowing us to organise it and to all the players and their wives and partners for coming over to Ireland.The two events in Ireland raised £100,000 and we are especially grateful to Fergus Slattery for his massive contribution with the Dublin Event. We are now pleased to announce that Wooden Spoon is finally established in Ireland."

By Nick Purewal, Press Association Sport Ireland Rugby Union Correspondent

COMMENT
& FEATURES

In the Front Line
the Progress of James Slipper

by RAECHELLE INMAN

'In 2010 Slipper made his Test debut off the bench against England in Perth under difficult circumstances. He joined a Wallaby scrum that was under enormous pressure'

It was a big four days for Wallaby prop James Slipper: on 6 June 2014 he turned 25; on 7 June he played his fiftieth Test for Australia, turning out a blinding man-of-the-match performance in the scrum and all over the paddock; then on 9 June Slipper was named a vice-captain of his country. That's a lot for someone so young to achieve, but Slipper takes it all in his stride. 'It's been a bit of a

whirlwind to be honest. Playing 50 games for my country is something I've been honoured to do. It is extremely humbling,' said Slipper.

He earned his fiftieth cap at Brisbane's Suncorp Stadium in front of his family and friends. At this milestone he joined an elite group of props including Al Baxter (69 games), Benn Robinson (66), Ben Alexander (62) and current Wallaby coach Ewen McKenzie (51).

This critical member of the Wallabies line-up has been the most regular starter of late. He doesn't get the accolades, he's not a try-scoring machine, but he's stable, consistent and the kind of player any side would envy. And those qualities have been recognised, elevating him to the leadership group. 'I never set out or aim to be a captain or vice-captain or leader for the Wallabies or Queensland it's just the way I play the game ... I'm not one for big speeches or one who rolls out the big motivational techniques, I'm a lead by example type of player, head down, do my job and do my job well and obviously Link [Ewen McKenzie] has seen something positive in that the players can follow,' he said.

'It brings another aspect when we're reviewing and making decisions. I'm in the tight five so it gives them a view of what we're thinking up front.'

Upon Slipper's appointment to the leadership role, McKenzie commented: 'I was really pleased with the contributions Adam Ashley-Cooper made to this group as vice-captain and I'm confident James Slipper will also step up to have a similar impact.

'James has already demonstrated the capacity to lead by guiding the Queensland Reds to four victories from his five Super Rugby games as captain in 2013.

'He's also been one of Australia's most consistent performers across 50 Tests and is extremely well respected within the group.'

'Slips', as he is known, has the ability to play at both loose- and tight-head. This has been a major asset and contributed to the prop's rapid rise through the ranks of professional rugby.

A former Australian Under 20s Player of the Year, in 2010 Slipper moved swiftly from the Queensland Reds Academy to a debut in Super Rugby to playing in 13 out of 14 Tests for the Wallabies.

ABOVE James Slipper packs down alongside Tatafu Polota-Nau against France in his fifty-second Test for the Wallabies.

FACING PAGE 'Slips' celebrates his 34th-minute try for the Reds against the Force in Brisbane in April 2014.

His versatility meant he was a handy bench player at the highest level before cementing his starting spot. 'I am more comfortable at loose-head and I feel I play my better rugby as a No. 1. Through my junior career I tended to be a tight-head and for the last four years at the Reds I have played tight-head but for the Wallabies I have mainly played at loose-head.'

In 2010 Slipper made his Test debut off the bench against England in Perth under difficult circumstances. He joined a Wallaby scrum that was under enormous pressure. 'As a young bloke I was thrown into the deep end and I had to learn quickly so I learnt by getting beat up and dominated in the scrum. When you get "out-scrummed" you find ways to better yourself, so I learn though trial and error and I keep turning up,' he said of the steep learning curve.

He says scrummaging is the area he continually works to improve. 'You have to put blood, sweat and tears into it and keep packing those scrums. It's the experience that enables you to become a better scrummager.

'There's a war between the ears between both props, every scrum is different, no two are alike. You are always trying to outwit your opponent and that's the bit I really enjoy. You have to keep your opponent guessing like a game of chess. It's good fun and you have to do your homework on your opponent.

'England, France, Italy … basically all the northern hemisphere have a different mindset around the scrum to us. Not just the players, the whole country really gets behind the mentality of scrummaging and getting really physical with your opponents. They tend to really enjoy that whereas down here we like the ball movement and the quicker rugby. You've also got to take into account the weather up there, there's a lot more dropped balls so they have to be good at scrums so it's always a big challenge when you come up against England, France and Italy. They all target our scrum as a weakness and they come hard at us there. But over the last couple of years we have improved a lot,' he said with tremendous enthusiasm.

He cites most-capped All Black prop Tony Woodcock as an inspiration. 'It's so much hard work to get to 50 Tests so you've really got to credit a man who gets to 100, especially as a front-rower. He's so resilient and has been playing for so many years he's a bloke I look up to.'

In his maiden year with the Wallabies, Slipper featured in the final 59 minutes of their dramatic 41-39 win over the Springboks at Bloemfontein, Australia's first win on the highveld in the Republic

for 47 years. He was part of the side that beat the All Blacks in Hong Kong and he ended the season as Australia's starting loose-head prop in the remarkable 59-16 annihilation of the then Six Nations champions France in Paris.

James shone in his second season of Super Rugby in 2011, playing an instrumental role in 14 games in the Reds' championship-winning campaign. But an ankle injury – syndesmosis – in the final regular-season game ruled him out of the semi-final and final successes. He also missed out on the Wallabies' first Tri-Nations title for a decade.

He made it back in time to feature in all seven matches played by Australia at his first Rugby World Cup in New Zealand. 'I played around 70 minutes off the bench in the Rugby World Cup semi-final against the All Blacks at Eden Park and, even though we ended up losing the game convincingly, it was a special moment for me.'

Slipper was Australia's starting loose-head during the wins over the Barbarians and Wales on the 2011 Spring Tour. He was the Queensland Reds' stand-out performer in 2012, not missing a single game and becoming just the second prop in Queensland rugby history to win the prestigious Pilecki Medal, awarded to the Players' Player of the Year.

FACNG PAGE James Slipper tries to evade Springbok lock Eben Etzebeth at Brisbane in The Rugby Championship 2013.

BELOW Auckland 2011. Slipper celebrates with Rob Simmons and fans after Australia's 32-6 RWC win over Italy.

Slipper's record 272 Pilecki Medal votes surpassed the previous mark set by Will Genia in 2011. He polled in the top three for eight matches during the season, including four of the last five critical rounds of the regular competition.

He was then selected in the Australia side which played against the British & Irish Lions, before being picked in McKenzie's Wallabies squads for The Rugby Championship and Spring Tour. He had really established himself by 2013, as one of six players who featured in all 15 matches played by the Wallabies.

What catches the eye with this prop is his unique ball skills and his proud running game: he is a front-rower with hands like a back. He opened the 2014 Australian winter Test campaign as a key link between

the forwards and backs in the Wallabies' seven-try demolition of France. He was mobile, having 'trimmed up a bit' in weight from 117kg to 113kg and he looked comfortable making yards alongside electric backs like Israel Folau. Slipper started all three matches in Australia's 3-0 series win, earning man-of-the-match honours in the second Test at Melbourne.

'Playing loose-head gives me a bit of freedom around the scrum as the tight-head does most of the work in the scrum and I steer it so I save a bit of energy so it gives me the opportunity to get around the field a bit more. I have put my hand up to do a bit more work, picking up the slack that I don't do in the scrum.'

Slipper wasn't always a front-rower. 'I started rugby in primary school at five-eighth [No. 10] and gradually moved up into the forwards as I got bigger and bigger.

'It wasn't until grade 12 that I started to play prop so it has been an interesting evolution so I'm happy where I'm at now, it's been a good journey.

'I love being involved in the game, whatever is needed of me … I really enjoy my defence, tackling … with the skills I have always had them so I like using them.

'At training I really like throwing the ball around, it's something I will always keep working on.'

His goal is 'to play the best rugby I can for Queensland and my country' and he is keen to play in two more World Cups. He is adamant he won't be playing top-level rugby until he's 40, claiming that with the heavy load of running and tackling he does he already feels ten years older than he is.

The parochial Queenslander was born and raised on the stunning Gold Coast and spends as much time back there as he can, surfing with his mates and his two brothers.

'The beach is number one outside of rugby. The day after a Reds home game I always head to the Gold Coast or Byron just to hang out and do a bit of surfing and relaxing. I'm just happy to be out there in the water … it's a good way to get away from rugby. It's good for the body and good for the head and all my life I've been at the beach with my mates so it's pretty natural to me.'

When he's not playing rugby or surfing, he is studying. Having already tried his hand at engineering and architecture, he has opted to focus on a business degree from the Queensland University of Technology. If Slipper is able to remain injury-free, he will continue to be a staple for the Wallabies. While his role is not a glamorous one, Slipper's ability to remain consistent is critical to the Wallabies' future success.

CRAFTED

FOR THE

MOMENT

SINCE 1799

17 99

GREENE KING
BURY ST EDMUNDS

IPA

HANDCRAFTED INDIA PALE ALE

greenekingipa.co.uk

Rugby and More
the Diary of Twickenham Stadium
by HUGH GODWIN

'The "non-rugby" events used to be confined to the annual Watchtower Convention of Jehovah's Witnesses. A sea change was signalled in 1999'

It was an arresting sight, in more than one sense, for the drivers arriving at the Harlequins v Bath match on the last day of the Aviva Premiership's regular league programme on the second Saturday in May. Pootling along the A316 with our heads full of simple thoughts of which of the two clubs would qualify for the title-deciding play-offs, we were brought to a halt at the traffic lights next to Twickenham Stadium to allow a bizarre-looking throng its passage to the day's other rugby event. Here, a zombie, there a man carrying – no, wearing – a cardboard coffin; everywhere a

startling collection of students and stag-do attendees done up in fancy dress as Minions from *Despicable Me* and every possible member of the animal kingdom, including Bugs Bunny, and less than matronly-looking nurses, with white cotton aprons spattered in fake blood.

To borrow from the old joke: 'Why did the Vincent Price-esque Dracula lookalike cross the road? To get to the monster-themed London Sevens, of course.' And if some of the Harlequins-bound spectators may have been moved to observe with a haughty sniff that 'they'll let anyone into Twickenham these days', the gathering of a world-record crowd for a single day of Sevens of 74,969 (most of them, it must be said, clothed as soberly as anyone at the Stoop) obliged anyone of a curious mind to wonder at the modern-day attractions and varying uses of England's national rugby stadium.

When Twickenham was described in the Rugby Football Union's *Centenary History* published in 1971 as the 'nerve centre' of the union and the game, it was as much administrative as physically active. The number of annual events making use of the pitch has more than doubled in the meantime to up to 25 each year. Some of these are familiar staples of the rugby calendar: Twickenham has been home to the England team since 1910 – although there are more matches than there used to be, with the autumn international series beginning in earnest only in the late 1990s – while the first Army v Navy match at the ground was played in 1920 and the Oxford v Cambridge Varsity Match arrived the following year. This year's Army v Navy match was watched by a crowd of just under 80,000, who saw the redoubtable prop Chris Budgen burrow to a popular try and the Bath and soon to be England squad wing Semesa Rokoduguni score another to help the Army to a 30-17 win. Other more recent additions have included the Premiership play-off final each May, the London Double Header in September and the Big Game staged by Harlequins at Christmas time. (Quins, as sub-tenants of the stadium from its inception in 1909, played 760 home matches on the ground up to 1990, but it has taken leagues and the open era to entice the kind of 74,000-plus crowd who watched their Big Game 6 versus Exeter Chiefs last December.)

There is the NatWest Schools Cup day of Under 18 and Under 15 finals (Dulwich College won their third Under 18 Cup title in a row this year), and the three RFU Cup competitions for clubs at level seven and below, which were all won in 2014 by teams from the Southwest – from the bottom up, as it were, Longlevens in the RFU Junior Vase, Newent supported by their 'Green Army' in the Senior Vase, and Trowbridge in the Intermediate Cup. And so it goes on, rugby-wise, with the BUCS student championship finals for men and women, re-timed and rebranded in 2014 as the 'Friday Night Lights' – Hartpury and Cardiff Metropolitan, respectively, were the winners. The annual England XV v Barbarians fixture in early June was bracketed with a trio of county finals, as Lancashire, Kent and Surrey won the three tiers of the County Championship (respectively the Bill Beaumont Cup, the Division 2 Plate, and the Shield). And the second and concluding day of the London Sevens – a family-oriented gathering as opposed to the overly boozy antics of the day before – saw New Zealand win both the individual tournament and the overall 2013-14 HSBC World Series.

As Richard Knight, the Rugby Football Union's stadium director since 2001, explained, the installation of a Desso pitch, laid in 2012, has allowed this increase in rugby activity. 'We always wanted Twickenham to be more heavily utilised,' Knight said. 'In addition to the 365-day use of the

hotel, gym and conference facilities, some of our rugby days can run to four 15-a-side matches, or a full programme of Sevens. On three occasions last season we were able to stage a women's international or a Sevens game straight after an England men's match. That is possible because we have a pitch that is three per cent artificial – or to put it another way, there are more than a million strands of artificial grass. It shows how technology supports what we're trying to achieve. It's always a case of striking a balance between rugby events, non-rugby events and pitch maintenance.'

The 'non-rugby' events used to be confined to the annual Watchtower Convention of Jehovah's Witnesses, which has proceeded unfussily at Twickenham over three days each summer for six decades. A sea change was signalled in 1999 when the RFU applied unsuccessfully for planning permission to host a concert by Luciano Pavarotti. The coming closure of Wembley Stadium for rebuilding represented the ideal chance to throw Twickenham open to music lovers in the summer months. The local planners quoted an 'unacceptable level of disturbance and inconvenience to residents', and the king of the aria was switched to Earls Court. But while the RFU were denied their tenor on that occasion, they have been sweating their biggest asset to the tune of millions of pounds almost ever since; when Rihanna performed to more than 100,000 fans over two nights, in June 2013, it was the latest of 23 concerts hosted at Twickenham in the past 11 years.

Mick Jagger and friends got the stone rolling, as it were, in 2003, and the old stagers have been followed onto English rugby's most hallowed turf by many other big-name acts: U2 in 2005, Eagles in 2006, The Rolling Stones again in August 2007, and on through The Police, Genesis, REM, Bon Jovi and Lady Gaga and her adoring 'Little Monsters' in September 2012. Where Pavarotti was once turned away, Iron Maiden have now been allowed in. There have also been charity fund-raisers: Robbie Williams headlined the Help for Heroes concert in September 2010, while in June 2013 came a concert by Chime For Change, which campaigns for women's and girls' health, education and

The Captain Departs
Steve Borthwick Bows Out
by CHRIS JONES

'Lesser men would have sat out the last two matches of a very long final season, but Borthwick ignored the pain of a shoulder problem and put his body on the line for his mates'

Jonny Wilkinson was given a double celebration to round off a remarkable rugby career with the Top 14 and Heineken Cup triumphs. For Steve Borthwick, the England and Saracens captain, there was only double despair as his remarkable 16 years of second-row graft came to a halt.

Borthwick's team-mates at Saracens were desperate to mark the end of his career with some silverware and having finished nine points clear at the top of the Aviva Premiership and learnt the painful lessons of semi-final losses the previous season in the Heineken Cup and domestic league,

this was surely going to be the North London club's year – wasn't it?

Unfortunately, Toulon proved too good for Sarries in the Heineken Cup final in Cardiff, while Northampton Saints won the Premiership title at Twickenham to leave Borthwick to reflect on a career finale that was both physically and mentally painful. Lesser men would have sat out the last two matches of a very long final season, but Borthwick ignored the pain of a shoulder problem and put his body on the line for his mates – something that he had always done while wearing the colours of Bath, Sarries and England.

While Wilkinson became a national icon during his career thanks to that World Cup-winning dropped goal, Borthwick was happy to have the adulation and respect of his fellow players – something Wilkinson also attracted. Borthwick never courted publicity, was rather uncomfortable when thrust into the spotlight and always looked for positives even when his team – particularly during his period as England captain – failed to hit the required playing standards. Borthwick always transferred criticism of the team onto himself, and this selfless attitude made him incredibly popular in the dressing room.

Those who have been captained by Borthwick rate him as one of the very best leaders they have ever followed.

Borthwick was capped 57 times by England and captained his country 21 times – mostly under Martin Johnson –

and Sarries wanted him to accept another contract at the end of last season, but the Cumbrian-born 34-year-old who led the club to a first Premiership triumph in 2011 wanted to quit on his terms, particularly as he was playing as strongly as ever.

He explained. 'Sarries asked me last March if I would sign a one-year contract and keep playing after this season and I thought long and hard about my decision. At the end of September I told the club "Thanks but I am going to retire at the end of this season." There are a few reasons: I didn't want my level of performance to drop and I wanted to make sure that I retired on my terms, playing well and being fit and healthy.

'I believe it's the right time to retire and very few players have the opportunity to make a decision – to say "I am going to finish on my terms" – rather than when someone says they don't want you anymore. Rugby is a very demanding sport and takes a toll on your body and it's a factor as well because you want to be in a good shape later on in life. I realise very few players get the opportunity I have been given.'

Borthwick has had considerable experience of dealing with disappointments and pressure in a career that brought him the ultimate honour of captaining his country, but also incredible flak when results went the wrong way.

Borthwick left Bath to join Sarries in 2007-08 when Eddie Jones, now Japan coach, convinced him to join the North London club's revolution. It coincided with Borthwick's mounting frustration about the direction Bath were taking and the promises that had not been kept and even now, he insists on sidestepping the exact details, preferring to accentuate the positives rather than the negative periods of his career.

That includes his time as England captain under Johnson, a regime that eventually imploded after the failed 2011 Rugby World Cup campaign which did not include Borthwick, whose Test career came to an end the previous year. 'There were some things around the England squad that weren't being done as well as they could have been and that came to light after I left the squad,' said

ABOVE Borthwick leading out
England at Christchurch in 2008
as tour captain to New Zealand.
Later that year, Borthwick
became full-time England captain
under Martin Johnson.

FACING PAGE Steve Borthwick of
Bath, Saracens and England.

Borthwick, who came close to making the 2003 World Cup-winning squad and believes he didn't make the most of his opportunities when involved in the 2007 cup campaign. 'Not making the 2003 squad was an incredibly tough blow, but it helped make me who I am. I always believe the team comes first and when you are England captain you have to deal with the pressure.'

Rugby is going to feature strongly in his future plans which also involve making the most of the master's degree he completed at the University of Hertfordshire. Time spent with various business leaders has fired his interest in this career option, while working as a line-out expert with the Japan RFU, helping Jones prepare the team, has also convinced Borthwick that coaching is the natural next step. He will be at Jones's side at the Rugby World Cup in England next year. Success with Japan will raise his coaching profile and as a brilliant technician he is certain to be in great demand when teams in England come to reassess their coaching set-ups in the coming season.

Of course, a return to Sarries in a coaching capacity would seem to be a natural step and the experience Borthwick will gain in Japan will be invaluable. Working with Jones will help Borthwick broaden his understanding of coaching at the highest level, while the former Wallaby head coach's ease in dealing with the media should also rub off on the big second-row.

After taking so many hits on his nose, there will also be time for Borthwick to get that area of his face finally straightened and fixed now that he will no longer be putting himself in harm's way. For years, he had a patch of skin that kept bleeding near the top of his nose and often lamented that there was no point in trying to sort out something permanent for that area while he was taking so much punishment!

'I have always been very goal-orientated and one I set of myself at 14-years-old was to play for England,' he added. 'I knew it may not happen, but promised myself it wouldn't be for a lack of trying. By doing that you earn respect from team-mates and coaches. Another goal was to be able to finish playing on my terms and that is what I am privileged to be able to do.'

Those are the heartfelt sentiments of a true rugby warrior and great leader.

No one knows *income* territory like our PROFIT hunters.

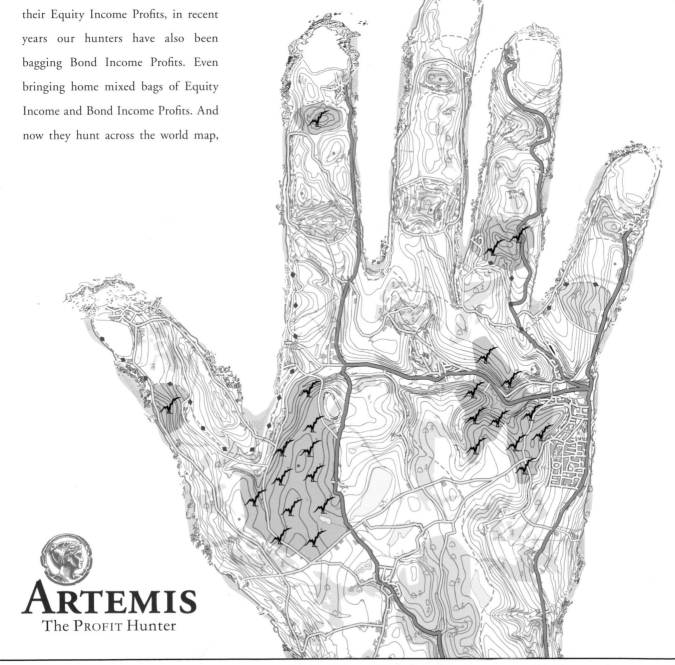

THE ARTEMIS income hunters are experts in their field. Indeed they know income territory like the proverbial back of their hand. Long famed for their Equity Income Profits, in recent years our hunters have also been bagging Bond Income Profits. Even bringing home mixed bags of Equity Income and Bond Income Profits. And now they hunt across the world map, training their sights on the coveted Global Income Profit too. Please remember that past performance should not be seen as a guide to future performance. The value of an investment and any income from it can fall as well as rise as a result of market and currency fluctuations and you may not get back the amount originally invested.

ARTEMIS
The PROFIT Hunter

0800 092 2051   *investorsupport@artemisfunds.com*   **artemis.co.uk**

Issued by Artemis Fund Managers Limited which is authorised and regulated by the Financial Conduct Authority (www.fca.org.uk), 25 The North Colonnade, Canary Wharf, London E14 5HS. For your protection calls are usually recorded. Contains Ordnance Survey data © Crown copyright and database right 2014.

INTERNATIONAL SCENE

Moldova on the March
Big Steps Forward in Eastern Europe
by CHRIS THAU

'Rugby had been well established in the Romanian region of Moldova since the late 1940s. However, in what was then Soviet Moldova the game started in 1967'

Moldova's remarkable run in the qualifying rounds of the European Zone of RWC 2015 and their presence among the top 30 nations in the IRB rankings defies both their brief rugby history and scarce playing resources. They are now twenty-ninth in the world rankings, having dropped four places from their highest ever position of twenty-fifth, reached in April this year after a successful run in the European Nations Cup (ENC) Division 1B.

'It is absolutely amazing to realise that all this has been achieved with a pool of less than 200-250 senior players, of which a substantial number play abroad. Those boys must be given credit for their hard work and dedication, against overwhelming odds, and of course one has to mention the efforts of the federation and their president Vasile Revenko, who was a former international player and national coach,' observed consultant coach Mircea Paraschiv, a former scrum half and captain of Romania, who has been helping the Romanian-speaking team for several years.

Among the teams they battled in ENC this year was Poland, a country with far greater resources and playing history. With their formidable pack firing on all cylinders, the powerful Moldavians pounded their way to a well-deserved win by 21 points to 12 at the Municipal Stadium in Sieldce, some 100 kilometres east of Warsaw, at the beginning of April. From the outset, the Polish team, largely selected by coach Marek Plonka from the two leading northern clubs Gdansk and Gdynia, engaged in battle up front, trying to out-muscle their guests, with their skipper, hooker Kamil

Bobryk of the French club Vienne, leading from the front. To an extent they surprised their visitors with the vivacity of their challenge, but stiff Moldavian tackling thwarted most of Poland's attacking ploys.

In the second half, the enormous pressure generated by the Moldavian pack – led by skipper Veaceslav Titica and spearheaded by the two Cobilas brothers, the loose-head Maxim, plying his trade for one of the Russian clubs in Krasnoyarsk, and tight-head Vadim, a regular with England's Sale Sharks – tipped the balance in the final stages of an absorbing battle. In addition to a first-half try touched down by their dynamic No. 8 Oleg Prepelita, the Moldavian forwards scored two more tries – the first through their bruising flanker Maxim Gargalac, and the second a penalty try following a series of collapsed scrums near the Polish line. All three tries were converted by the new Moldavian outside half, English-born Craig Felston, a graduate in sports science from Kingston University. Felston found out that a great-grandfather had come to England from Moldova and promptly wrote to the Moldova federation, who were desperately looking for a good kicking fly half to play behind their dominant pack.

'The federation president Vasile Revenko had a look at my CV and after checking my eligibility invited me over to Chisinau for a trial. The first time I wore the Moldova jersey was in Sevens against Sweden in a Tel Aviv tournament, and I was so excited, it was the proudest moment of my life. It was then very fitting that my first full international was against Sweden as well. To be honest, for all this to come true was out of this world.

'I tried to learn as much useful Romanian vocabulary as possible but there are some very good English speakers in the team so whenever there is a problem they will help. The boys have accepted me and have never felt any animosity towards me for being a "foreigner". Besides Mircea Paraschiv our main coach speaks very good English. He is a former Romanian scrum half, captain and coach so his experience is very beneficial for us as a team.'

There are two territories named Moldova, located on either side of the Prut River in Eastern Europe. They are both inhabited by the same Romanian-speaking population, though one of the territories, the eastern, has got a significant Russian-speaking minority. Originally part of the same medieval Principality of Moldova, the two have been split apart by war, ideology and geopolitics. The last time the two parts of Moldova were together was before the Second World War, when they were both a region of Romania. The western portion is still part of Romania and is located between the Carpathian Mountains and the Prut, while the other is the Republic of Moldova, an independent state, which broke away from the former Soviet Union.

ABOVE Centre Andrei Baltag, supported by Craig Felston, on the attack against Poland.

FACING PAGE The formidable Moldova front row prepares to pack down in the Polish game. From left to right: Vadim Cobilas, Dumitru Vasilachi and Maxim Cobilas.

This latter territory, most of which sits between the rivers Prut and Dniester, used to host the huge military conglomerate of the 14th Soviet Army facing the eastern flank of NATO, which had dramatic consequences for its demography as well as the politics of the country when it became independent once again in 1991. A year later, the year the Moldova Rugby Federation was formed, a short and vicious civil war led to the de facto division of the country into the Republic of Moldova and the Russian-speaking autonomous region of Transnistria, a process quite similar to what is going on in Eastern Ukraine right now.

Rugby had been well established in the Romanian region of Moldova since the late 1940s. However, in what was then Soviet Moldova the game started in 1967, with the arrival at the Technical University of Chisinau of two young rugby missionaries from Odessa – Dima Seltzer and Vladimir Blizniuc. In a surprisingly short time, the two managed to get a team started by attracting players, mostly students, from other sports. The new club, Politechnica Chisinau, not only survived but also prospered for quite a while. One of the players at that time was Boris Iacob, who nearly 25 years later became the first president of the newly founded Moldova Rugby Federation. Those who believed that he would become just a kind of a presidential figurehead in the old style of the Soviet system were surprised by his energy and determination to help the game expand.

'At the first meeting, I told them that rugby was too small to survive in the country with a playing base of about 100 players and that we needed to expand. In 1992 we joined the European body,

ABOVE Moldova Rugby Federation president Boris Iacob (left) with John Broadfoot of the rugby charity SOS Moldova (centre) and an official of the Moldova Rugby Federation.

RIGHT The Moldova national team that played Poland in April 2014.

FIRA-AER. In fact it was Romania who presented our application at the Paris meeting, as we did not have money to travel. The civil war split our small rugby family even further, as one of our leading clubs from Tiraspol broke away. But after a while, thanks to rugby and the good relationship I had with Nikolai Kaziuk – the coach and manager of Olympic Tiraspol, with whom I played during the days of Politechnica Chisinau – we managed to find a common language and somehow safeguard Moldavian rugby. In 1994 we joined the IRB and started to work on development.

'We signed contracts with PE teachers and some of the players of the national team to teach the kids the basics and then coach them. We have been supported by the Education Ministry and the Department for Education of the City of Chisinau. The results speak for themselves. From a player base of about 150 in 1995, we have now about 3000 players of all ages, from senior, to youth and minis – a 2000 per cent increase,' Mr Iacob said.

Moldova's scrum anchorman is Vadim Cobilas, the Sale Sharks tight-head, who has made a special effort to be available for his country's international matches; unlike some of his fellow East European players who tend to forget where they come from when they touch fame and wealth in the West. 'From the outset I told Steve Diamond, the Sale coach, who brought me to England, that whenever possible I want to be released to play for Moldova. I wanted to be honest from the outset because playing for Moldova was something that was important to me. To his credit, he understood my way of thinking and has been very good to release me whenever possible.

'I started playing rugby at 19, which is quite late, having done Greco-Roman wrestling in my youth. I was at the PE Institute in Chisinau, and felt I was going nowhere with my wrestling, when my friend Veaceslav Titica, who is now the captain of the national team, asked me to try my hand at rugby. I tried and loved it! Next I was playing for the country, which was a great honour and incentive and I was offered a contract by the then leading Russian club Gagarin Air Academy in Monino.

'We are the same small group of players who put Moldova on the rugby map and when my young brother Maxim joined us, after spending some time in Romania, things got even better. Having been together for such a long time we are now playing quite well together having gelled over the years, which is a significant factor in our current success story. This is the main reason for our very good run of success in the ENC when suddenly we found ourselves in the headlines, playing in the RWC qualifying rounds. It is a shame that we did not score the fourth try against Poland, which would have secured us a bonus point, but to be honest, this was a very good win against a very strong and well-respected team. What is important now is to use these opportunities to strengthen the game in Moldova, to enable the next generation to come to the fore. This is why these high-profile games, like the one we played at the weekend in the qualifying rounds of RWC 2015, are so important to us.'

justice. Madonna was a presenter that night, Prince Harry sent a videotaped message of best wishes, and the performers who helped raise £2.8 million included Beyoncé, Florence and the Machine and Jessie J.

It all adds up to an eclectic crowd, with differing views of what Twickenham stands for. Any of them entering the West Car Park may glance up at the statue of a lion on top of the gates. It was a gift from the Greater London Council in 1971, but it was a relic, itself, from the old Lion Brewery on the South Bank that closed in 1947. Salvaged and painted in gold, it stands guard now outside a stadium of 82,000 seats and countless individual memories. As Matthew Howard, the Trowbridge RFC captain, put it on the day of his club's Intermediate Cup win, 'For any amateur, to run out at Twickenham is a once in a lifetime opportunity.' Early in 2014, girls from two Oxfordshire rugby clubs played a curtain-raiser to England's Six Nations Championship match against Ireland. Among them was nine-year-old Alice Hipkiss, a survivor of a heart transplant in 2008. All sections of Alice's club, the Gosford All Blacks, carry a logo, 'Transplants save lives', on their playing shirts. Alice's father David reported his daughter as being 'naturally, thrilled to be playing on the pitch – almost as much as I was to be watching her!'

There were no concerts this past summer, during a shutdown for construction work as part of a £75-million programme to refurbish the stadium and make it fit for the 2015 Rugby World Cup and the 25 years beyond. New big screens, Wi-Fi provision for spectators and a revamped World Rugby Museum containing 25,000 artefacts are among the many items on the ongoing schedule of works. But the stadium reopened in August for the Jehovah's Witnesses and the much newer congregation of the World Club Sevens, an experimental competition in only its second year.

The Chime For Change event featured a duet of Jennifer Lopez and Mary J. Blige singing The Beatles' 'Come Together'. It could serve as a theme for the modern-day Twickenham; gradually rebuilt and embellished, its ambience will always divide opinion, but it is undeniably a place of pilgrimage in many different ways.

England Back to Back
the 2014 Junior World Championship
by ALAN LORIMER

'Yes, England had height, weight and power in their forward pack and muscularity behind the scrum, but what will be remembered is their ball skills'

After years when it seemed New Zealand were untouchable in age-grade rugby, England made an emphatic statement about the northern hemisphere game by winning their second successive title in the Auckland-staged IRB Junior World Championship last June with victory by the slenderest of margins over South Africa in the final at Eden Park. England missed out on the 2014 Six Nations Under 20 title, but when it came to the global competition their all-round firepower proved deadly and confirms that the Premiership Academies' competitive environment, with its advanced conditioning programmes, together with an integrated approach throughout all the England age teams represent a winning formula.

That structure of course is mirrored in South Africa and New Zealand and to a large extent in Australia, France, Wales and Ireland. What England have done is to maximise their advantage of a large pool of players, making sure that they are physically and mentally prepared to conquer the best in the world.

What was appealing about this England team was the ball-playing ability in every position. Yes, England had height, weight and power in their forward pack and muscularity behind the scrum, but

ABOVE England Under 20 are junior world champions for the second year in a row after beating South Africa 21-20.

what will be remembered is their ball skills. And no more so than in the semi-final against Ireland when England gave full expression to these skills, with soft hands from props, basketball handling from the back five and sublime touches from the inside backs, including Fiji-style flipping the ball between the legs.

England, with power, pace and precision and an evident desire to enjoy their rugby, had the game won by half-time when they led 34-3 with spectacular tries that included top-drawer touchdowns from prop Danny Hobbs-Awoyemi – with help from fellow prop Paul Hill – and from winger Howard Packman after a finely judged cross-kick by fly half Billy Burns.

Arguably South Africa had a much tougher route to the final than England, having had to play New Zealand in the pool stages and again in the second of the semi-finals. In that penultimate-round match New Zealand looked on course to book their place in the final when they led 25-20 with 13 minutes of the game left, only for 16½-stone centre André Esterhuizen to power through two tackles for an unconverted try in the corner.

Esterhuizen had been yellow-carded in the first half for a high tackle and was fortunate to have remained on the field after a dangerous aerial challenge after the break. His try levelled the scores and it was left to hooker Corniel Els to grab the winner.

And so to the final at Eden Park. England were undoubtedly the more nervous of the two sides, and that appeared to manifest itself in a malfunctioning line out. In the event South Africa took advantage, turning possession into points through a penalty by IRB Junior Player of the Year Handré Pollard and the fly half's conversion of a try by centre Jesse Kriel, whose twin brother, Dan, was on the wing.

England had kept in touch with a penalty by fly half Billy Burns, but it was to be a monster goal from six metres inside the England half by full back Aaron Morris that arguably won the match. The contribution by Morris appeared to act as a spur for England, who produced a potent attack in which centre Nick Tompkins did the damage to give their prolific scorer Nathan Earle a try in the corner for an 11-10 interval lead.

Burns and Pollard exchanged penalties early in the second half before back-row replacement Joel Conlon finished off an England drive to the line, Burns adding the conversion. Kriel then ran in for his second try, the conversion by Pollard bringing the Junior Boks within a point of England with the scoreline at 21-20. But that was to be the final score of the match. England, under coach Nick Walshe, had successfully defended the title they won in France. Southern hemisphere rugby had again come off second best.

Of course, the JWC is about more than winning the title. Resources and domestic systems will always determine the outcome at the top end, but what matters for all the countries taking part is the development of future senior international players – in which context England coach Stuart Lancaster will have noted a few players not far off a senior jersey. Impressive for England behind the scrum were centres Nick Tompkins and Harry Sloan, wingers Nathan Earle and Howard Packman and fly half Billy Burns. Up front the mobility of prop Danny Hobbs-Awoyemi and lock Maro Itoje made the pair stand-outs, while the back row of Gus Jones, Ross Moriarty and James Chisholm were solidity personified.

The Junior Boks while disappointed will be pleased that their production line appears to be churning out talent. Handré Pollard has already experienced Super Rugby and will surely advance to greater things. Many fans warmed to the skills of winger Sergeal Petersen and full back Warrick Gelant and the maturity of locks JD Schickerling and Nico Janse Van Rensburg. Overall the impression is of a queue of young players knocking on the door of Springbok rugby.

Several pundits in New Zealand had declared pre-tournament that their 2014 squad was not as strong as in previous years. But the skills of players like full back Damian McKenzie, winger Tevita Li and fly half Richard Mo'unga certainly lit up the JWC.

New Zealand claimed third place after defeating Ireland 45-23 in the play-off. Ireland, however, did well to reach the top four, confirming that Irish rugby has got it right at age-grade level. Outstanding for Ireland was outside centre Garry Ringrose (already being tipped as a successor to Brian O'Driscoll), full back Cian Kelleher and fly half Ross Byrne.

Having been runners-up in the 2013 JWC, Wales dropped down the rankings to seventh place after finishing second in their pool to Ireland. Wales opened confidently with an easy 48-19 win over Fiji but then lost to Ireland 35-21 before reasserting themselves with a 13-3 win over France.

Then in the fifth-place semi-final the quirks of the JWC resulted in Wales and France meeting for a second time, and on this occasion France were the winners 19-18. But in the ensuing play-off Wales staged a recovery to snuff out a belligerent Samoa side with a 20-3 victory. Wales are never short of fly halves, and from their 2014 JWC squad Angus O'Brien added himself to the supply. There were fine displays too from wing Dafydd Howells (who scored against Fiji just seven seconds into the match), centres Steffan Hughes and Jack Dixon and No. 8 James Benjamin.

Meanwhile Six Nations Under 20 winners France were left to fight it out with Australia for fifth place, but it was not to be a *triomphe* for les Tricolores, who lost out to the young Wallabies 34-27 in an entertaining and largely inconsequential match.

For Scotland the 2014 JWC was always going to be a test of survival, drawn as they were alongside South Africa, New Zealand and Samoa in Pool C and moreover fielding a young squad. Twelve of the party will be eligible for the 2015 tournament, and three of these – flanker James Ritchie, fly half Rory Hutchinson and prop Zander Fagerson – for the 2016 championship. Scotland's perennial problem, though, is the shallow depth of age-grade rugby, in no small part due to the decline of competitive sport in state schools. The other handicap is the current absence of 'regional academies' in the mould of the Premiership set-up – resources that prepare the better players for the global challenge – resulting in a squad several of whom are just below the standard required.

At the conclusion of the pool matches, Scotland found themselves in familiar territory among the 9th-12th-ranked countries and facing Italy in a semi-final that had relegation implications. The Scots had lost to the young Azzurri in the Six Nations, but in the rematch at North Harbour it was Scotland who prevailed with a 21-18 win to retain their top-tier status. Then in the ninth-place play-off Scotland lost 41-21 to Argentina, resulting in the Scots yet again finishing in tenth position.

In the eleventh-place play-off Italy fended off Fiji, meaning that the Pacific islanders were relegated to the Junior World Rugby Trophy, swapping places with Japan for the 2015 JWC in Italy, where England will be bidding for a hat-trick of titles in the face of new-look South Africa and New Zealand squads, both doing their best to halt the men in white.

Namibia Through RWC 2015 Qualifying in Africa

by **CHRIS THAU**

'In the second match, hosts Madagascar, or "Les Makis" as they are called by their passionate fans, showed glimpses of the sublime skills that they are renowned for'

ABOVE The Webb Ellis Cup creates great excitement among young Madagascar fans.

We left it a bit late, but better late than never,' said a relieved Namibia captain PJ van Lill after his team's sensational comeback in the last match of the 2014 Africa Cup, which secured the Welwitschias the Africa 1 starting berth at the RWC 2015 finals in England. It was an astonishing outcome for a remarkable tournament held in the spectacular setting of the Mahamasina Stadium in Antananarivo, the capital city of Madagascar. The quality of the tournament and the standard of organisation speak volumes about the work the Confederation of African Rugby (CAR) and the IRB are doing in Africa.

'This was one of the most exciting CAR tournaments to date and the fact that we did not know the outcome until the last match shows how much the game has progressed in Africa,' said CAR President Abdelaziz Bougja. And he added, 'The standard of the game in Africa has gone up tremendously and the four teams produced spectacular encounters widely appreciated by the generous Malgache public. Congratulations to Namibia the winners and good luck to Zimbabwe in the RWC 2015 Repechage and of course a warm thank you to the Madagascar Rugby Federation President Marcel Rakotomalala and his team for putting together a great event.'

On the morning of the final day, Kenya, with the maximum ten points from two matches (eight tournament points for two wins and two offensive bonus points) were hot favourites to make history by winning the right to represent Africa at an RWC tournament finals for the first time ever. Even a defeat with a bonus point – either offensive (by scoring four or more tries) or defensive (by having seven or less points scored against) – would have secured Kenya the flight tickets for England 2015. The loose talk in the Kenyan camp about the celebrations organised for the prospective heroes in Nairobi the following week may have been their undoing, no matter how much Head Coach Jerome Paarwater must have tried to keep their minds concentrated on the match in hand. They did not, and paid dearly for it, finishing the tournament in third position.

Zimbabwe, their opponents in the final match, had amassed six tournament points from their previous two encounters – a win with an offensive bonus point v Madagascar (4+1) and a defeat with a defensive bonus point v Namibia (1). In order to win the tournament and the coveted RWC qualifying slot, not only had they to defeat Kenya with a bonus point but also deny them a bonus point. And with three tries under their belt, they had the opportunity to add a fourth a couple of minutes from the end, had they decided to either run the penalty awarded by South African referee Lourens van der Merwe or kick for touch near the Kenyan line and play it from there. For unknown reasons, the Sables bench counselled fly half Guy Cronjé to kick at goal rather than to touch, which added three more points to their tally but basically eliminated them from the gold-medal race. It was

a crass error of judgment, which let the Welwitschias through to England 2015, where they will join New Zealand, Argentina, Tonga and Georgia in Pool C of the tournament. Zimbabwe may still qualify to RWC 2015 via Russia and probably Uruguay in the Repechage, but that is a very long and arduous road, with no clear outcome in sight.

The Antananarivo tournament started with a bang, as Kenya managed to defeat favourites Namibia 29-22 in an exciting, action-packed game. Led by their athletic second-rower Wilson K'Opongo, Kenya managed to overcome a sluggish start, which saw them trailing by 12 points after some ten minutes of play, to score a crucial try just before half-time to close the gap to five points. Early in the game, they seemed to struggle in every department, with their scrummage in tatters, a disorganised line out and a porous defence. In the second half Kenya, coached by the experienced Western Province man Jerome Paarwater, sprang to life, scoring two tries in five minutes to take the lead, which half an hour earlier seemed beyond their abilities.

In the second half their scrummage absorbed and controlled the powerful Namibian surges, their back row challenged at the breakdown with a vengeance, and significantly their line out kicked into action. The lead changed hands three times, before Namibia battled back with full back Chrysander Botha going over for their third try and outside half Theuns Kotzé landing the conversion to level the score at 19-all. However, a further try by Sevens star Andrew Amonde rewarded Kenyan efforts with an offensive bonus point, fly half Lavin Asego adding the conversion for the final scoreline of 29-22.

'We just reminded everyone what we had to do, after a pretty poor first half, and that's what the boys did. I am really proud of them,' Paarwater said. The former Western Province back-row and Emerging Springboks forwards coach is the author of Kenya's upsurge in rugby fortunes, having replicated in the main game the highly successful Sevens programme that saw Kenya emerging among the elite of the short game. Paarwater, born into a rugby-mad family in Bellville, Western Province, in July 1966, was the fifth of the six rugby-playing sons of Jacobus and Rosina Paarwater, a leading family of anti-apartheid activists in the Western Cape. His father started the rugby club in

Home

Work

Legacy

Experiences

Passion

Family

Living

We focus on the most important economy in the world. Yours.

Your personal economy is always with you. But it's only when we step back and look at all the different aspects of your life, that we are able to see yours. It shows how your family, your home, your passions and your career are all intertwined. We see how it's unique to you and constantly changing. So at HSBC Premier our focus is on providing personal support, for your personal economy.

Find out more at hsbcpremier.com/personaleconomy

HSBC Premier is subject to financial elegibility criteria.

Proud supporter of the Wooden Spoon.

HSBC

Premier

Bellville that catered for non-whites, while his mother Rosina had the rugby stadium built in town; it now carries her name – Rosina Paarwater Stadium.

In the second match of the opening day, hosts Madagascar, or 'Les Makis' as they are called by their passionate fans, showing glimpses of the sublime skills that they are renowned for, fell to a powerful and pragmatic Zimbabwe 22-57 in an exciting match that kept the capacity crowd of 25,000 on their toes to the very end. If there were any doubts about the ability of the Sables, coached by former international wing forward Brendan Dawson, to handle the high-pace game played by the hosts, they dissipated them in emphatic fashion, by scoring eight tries against a team who at one stage early in the second half seemed quite capable of turning the tables on their guests. Had Madagascar scored a couple of tries earlier, when their flyers broke through the Sables defence, the outcome might have been different, observed CAR Tournament Director and IRB Regional Manager for Africa Jean-Luc Barthes. Indeed Madagascar's uncanny ability to manufacture tries out of thin air is simply bewildering. Under veteran coach Berthin Rafalimanana – 'the old wizard', as his disciples call him – the Makis play a breathtaking brand of rugby, which could bring them some valuable scalps if they could upgrade their forward platform and maintain both the pace and the intensity for the full 80 minutes, or if they put time and resources into the short game.

On day two of the tournament, it looked for quite a while as if Zimbabwe, who scored three well-taken tries, were going to put Namibia to the sword as well, but injuries to key forwards Sanele Sibanda and Jan Ferreira disrupted their ball-winning ability, and more significantly their composure. This was when Namibia coach Danie Vermeulen made an inspired substitution at scrum half, replacing Arthur Bower with the dynamic Eneill Buitendag, who injected pace, fluency and drive into what until then looked like a sluggish effort. Suddenly a resurgent Namibia swung into action and scored again to take the lead 24-20, but Zimbabwe defended grimly and managed to salvage a defensive bonus point, keeping their hopes of winning the 2014 Africa Cup alive.

On the final day, the least likely scenarios materialised, with both Kenya, a shadow of the team that inflicted such damage on Namibia in the opening match, and Zimbabwe, who simply misread the rules of the tournament, missing the boat. It was left to Namibia to pile nearly a ton of points on a brave but inadequate Madagascar in the final act of an amazing four-nation tournament to end an incredible journey from nowhere on day one to England 2015 on the last day. Madagascar battled bravely to the very end in order to present Coach Rafalimanana, who stepped down after the game, with a suitable farewell present, but it was not to be. Madagascar lock forward Jean de Dieu Rakotonirina, at 43 the oldest player in the tournament and possibly in RWC 2015, had also made his farewell appearance.

BELOW Pack the bags and start the car. Namibia are off to England after their 89-10 win over Madagascar brought them the Africa Cup and qualification for the finals of RWC 2015

The Group of Death
Pool A at RWC 2015

by CHRIS FOY

'However daunting a prospect Pool A appeared back then, it has since acquired an even more deadly look, given the fortunes of those countries involved'

As the countdown to the World Cup intensifies, there is no escaping the brutality of the top-heavy draw. The Group of Death will create major casualties – possibly too close to home for comfort. Initial intrigue at next year's tournament will overwhelmingly focus on Pool A, due to the log jam of primary nations in close proximity. Hosts England, bitter rivals Wales and resurgent Australia will all collide in the round-robin stages, with just two places in the knockout phase up for grabs.

It promises to be tense and ferocious and too close to call; all thanks to freak circumstances which conspired to create this overloaded group. When the draw was made in December 2012, England had slipped to fifth in the IRB rankings and Wales had just slumped to ninth, on the back of poor autumn results – leaving those sides among the second and third seeds respectively.

When the draw was made for the recent football World Cup, the FA chairman's response was an infamous, throat-slitting gesture, given the magnitude of what England faced. Ian Ritchie, the chief executive of the RFU, would have been forgiven for a similar reaction when the national team were condemned to a fraught pool campaign.

However daunting a prospect Pool A appeared back then, it has since acquired an even more deadly look, given the fortunes of those countries involved. Prior to this year's Rugby Championship in the southern hemisphere, Australia lay third in the world rankings, with England fourth and Wales sixth. Having three of the leading half-dozen rugby nations in one pool represents a colossal imbalance. That doesn't even convey the full story though. In late June, Fiji thrashed the Cook Islands 108-6 to confirm their place in the same elite group, and the Pacific island team are on an upward curve again after a dire campaign in 2011 – edging back up to eleventh in the rankings, having beaten Italy (25-14) earlier that month.

Their qualification is bound to ignite a sense of Welsh dread, based on the remarkable occasion in 2007 when Fiji scorched the Dragons in Nantes – winning an epic encounter 38-34 to knock their supposedly superior opponents out of the World Cup. That result led to Gareth Jenkins' demise as head coach the next morning. More recently, in 2010, Wales could only draw (16-16) with Fiji in Cardiff, so Warren Gatland will be alert to the unpredictable threat they pose.

Nevertheless, the anticipated three-way battle for quarter-final places from Pool A will dominate the agenda. In different ways, these countries have all shown their credentials as significant tournament challengers, let alone mere last-eight participants.

Take the hosts, to start with. Under Stuart Lancaster, there is the palpable sense of a sustained and fundamental building process. Layers are being added, step by painstaking step. First, a new squad was assembled and youth promoted. England quickly established a formidable team spirit and defensive resolve, before recognising their attacking limitations at the end of 2013 and setting out to become more dynamic, fluent and cohesive, to complement their considerable power.

There is growing choice in most positions too. Yet, the priorities for Lancaster now are

FACING PAGE Will Genia is charged down by England's Wood, Launchbury and Mako Vunipola at Twickenham in November 2013. England won this encounter 20-13.

RIGHT Line-out action from Fiji's 108-6 RWC Qualifying victory over Cook Islands in Lautoka. The win sealed their place in Pool A for England 2015.

consistency of selection and tangible momentum. A year out from their home World Cup, England are well aware that there is too much uncertainty about back-line personnel and also that they urgently need a run of victories or a Six Nations title to enhance belief in their ability to emulate the triumphant class of 2003.

For Wales, the scenario is a divided picture of success and failure, depending on the origins of their rivals. Gatland has overseen Grand Slams in 2008 and 2012, and a championship title in 2013, but his side have a lamentable record against the southern hemisphere giants – with just one victory set against 24 defeats. However, it has often been a tale of agonising, marginal failure. For instance, in ten Tests against Australia during Gatland's tenure, Wales have lost nine times, but eight of those nine defeats have been by single-figure margins. Summing up the so-near-but-so-far sequence were the 2012 losses in Melbourne, Sydney and Cardiff, by a combined tally of just five points. The Kiwi coach will hope that such heartbreak arms his men to turn the tables when it matters most.

In principle, England will benefit from home advantage at the World Cup, but the Welsh will be well supported and undaunted at Twickenham. They have won twice on their last three championship visits to southwest London, and also produced a record 30-3 demolition of their neighbours to prevent an English Grand Slam at the Millennium Stadium in 2013.

Months later, Australia were in a state of disarray as they were annihilated by the Lions in the series decider in Sydney, leading to the removal of head coach Robbie Deans. The Wallaby camp was blighted by indiscipline and brittle morale, while the presence of a handful of world-class players could not disguise the dearth of depth in several areas, especially up front. But much has changed since that watershed period. Ewen McKenzie has revived battered Australian self-belief and reasserted their forward play while also trusting in the instincts of his charismatic back-line figures. While some of the iconic attacking stars such as Will Genia, Quade Cooper and Kurtley Beale have endured turbulent times, Israel Folau has rapidly emerged as a world force from full back or wing, and the cross-code sensation is destined to illuminate the World Cup.

With Australian Super 15 sides prospering in the 2014 campaign, there is a mood of renewed optimism Down Under, despite the looming danger of a player exodus late next year. McKenzie's man-management skills will ensure the Wallabies arrive on these shores united, organised and highly motivated, and Australia have a proud pedigree in tournament rugby which they will be determined to maintain.

Predictions are a fool's game in this sort of scenario, but despite their near miss against the Springboks in Nelspruit back in June, Wales's problems against the southern elite may turn out to be the crucial factor. At this stage, it is reasonable to imagine that the results will reflect the rankings, with England and Australia progressing – but perhaps in that order, with the hosts capable of trumping the Wallabies at home to top Pool A.

Elsewhere, each of the remaining three pools will provide their own intrigue. In Pool B, South Africa should beat all-comers, but Samoa will challenge Scotland strongly for the runners-up place and Japan are rising fast under Eddie Jones. The Brave Blossoms ambushed Wales at home in 2013 and after breaking into the world's top ten, they could take a significant scalp next year.

In Pool C, the All Blacks will face minimal resistance – which may count against them in the latter stages. Argentina have plunged down the rankings since their glorious peak in 2007, leaving the Pumas to fend off dangerous Tonga and Georgia for the second qualifying spot. The East European nation beat Samoa last November and their trademark forward clout will trouble their rivals.

Finally in Pool D, it appears to be a straight tussle between Ireland and France to settle the two qualification places. Joe Schmidt can turn the Irish into semi-final contenders on the back of his success with Leinster, while Philippe Saint-André continues to endure all manner of indignities trying to make Les Bleus competitive in the face of what he regards as a lack of co-operation from the Top 14 clubs. Italy, Canada and Romania are destined to make up the numbers.

What is most heartening for the global game is that – thanks to more regular, meaningful competition and a balanced pool schedule – the Tier Two nations should be able to make a greater impact this time. Samoa are best equipped to carry the flag for the traditional underdogs into the quarter-finals, which could look like this: South Africa (B1) v Australia (A2), New Zealand (C1) v France (D2), Ireland (D1) v Argentina (C2), England (A1) v Samoa (B2).

FACING PAGE Graham Dewes scores the match-winning try for Fiji against Wales in Nantes in Pool B of RWC 2007.

BELOW Adam Ashley-Cooper touches down for one of his two tries that helped bring the 2014 Super Rugby title to Australia, as the Waratahs beat the Crusaders of New Zealand 33-32 in the final.

Sevens On the Rise
the Women's Short Form Takeover

by **SARA ORCHARD**

'The first countries to go full-time were the Netherlands and Canada. They've been followed by Australia, the USA, Ireland, Spain, Russia and New Zealand'

Revolution or evolution? Whatever you want to call it, the face of women's rugby is changing. We can all feel the 2016 Rio Olympics closing in and countries across the globe are opening their eyes to the possibilities that rugby Sevens offers.

The lure of international broadcast coverage and attracting print media interest is winning over governing bodies worldwide. No prizes for guessing that the side leading the women's Sevens charge is New Zealand's Black Ferns. They've retained their Sevens World Series title in 2014 by

winning three out of the five legs of the series, but the Australians pushed them hard.

Black Ferns fly half Kelly Brazier knows. 'It was a huge achievement – it's always harder to keep winning and to stay at the top than it is to chase. But two years out from the Olympics I think we're in a pretty good place at the moment.'

Being at the top of world rugby is what New Zealand are used to and the new Olympic stage is something Brazier and her team are fast adapting to. 'Sevens will probably lead the way for women now – because for us it's now semi-professional, and with Sevens in the Olympics, Sevens will have a greater global reach.'

Brazier's words are a brutal statement for rugby purists who live and die for Fifteens, but for women, Sevens is offering far, far more.

Many Sevens nations now have full- or part-time women's programmes. It does raise eyebrows, but the first countries to go full-time were the Netherlands and Canada – neither considered rugby powerhouses, but clearly opportunists. They've been followed by Australia, the USA, Ireland, Spain, Russia and New Zealand.

The Australian Women, known as the Wallaroos, now boast the IRB Women's Sevens Player of the Year, Emilee Cherry. She's one of Australia's 20 full-time female players and has never played Fifteens, having converted from being a Touch Football player. She helped her country to lift the two WSWS titles New Zealand failed to win, Dubai and São Paulo.

The 21-year-old Cherry admits to being blown away by her accolade. 'I was extremely humbled and taken aback after being named the IRB Women's Player of the Year. As a team we had a phenomenal season and the accolade I received was off the back of all their hard work.

'One of my favourite quotes of all time – and my Mum has always reminded me of this – is: "I never said it would be easy, I said it would be worth it". This really rung true this season.'

ABOVE Kelly Brazier of the Black Ferns on the break during the first Test v England at Auckland in July 2013. Brazier features in the New Zealand Sevens and Fifteens squads.

FACING PAGE Heather Fisher of England evades the Netherlands' Anne Hielckert at the 2014 Amsterdam WSWS event. The Netherlands were one of the first countries to have a full-time women's Sevens set-up.

The rise of Australia has been the stand-out performance over the 2013-14 season. The consequence sees their rivalry with New Zealand intensify, but Cherry feels it's never changed. 'There is always going to be a trans-Tasman rivalry in any sport and rugby is no different. New Zealand are ranked number one across every form of the game – whether it be Fifteens or Sevens – so whenever you come up against them it is always going to be the toughest game.

'We faced them in four out of the five tournament finals in the series which created quite the contest, with both of the teams knowing that there was much more on the line than the tournament win.'

Other nations are keen to make their mark on the rugby Sevens landscape with the Olympic carrot seen as the incentive. The Netherlands Women's head coach Chris Lane looks after 18 full-time Dutch players. 'Here in the Netherlands we have a full-time Sevens programme. As well as talented athletes you need money to run these programmes and without the Olympic partnerships this would not be possible.

'There is a greater awareness of rugby as a women's sport now, with many athletes from other sports wanting to give rugby a go and chase their own Olympic dreams.'

In Lane's opinion the Olympics represents 'The biggest achievement available to any athlete'.

The IRB are also aware of this lure. In 2014 they announced that the next instalment of the Women's Rugby World Cup (the Fifteens competition) will be held in 2017 rather than 2018 to avoid a clash with the Sevens World Cup. The theory is that if both tournaments ran in the same year, the Fifteens would see a dramatic dip in the quality of play, with individuals opting to prioritise the more high-profile and potentially financially rewarding Sevens.

IRB Women's Development Manager Su Carty explains that the change should allow players more opportunities to play both formats. 'We are committed to ensuring the best-possible competition schedule for our players. Many of our Fifteens stars play Sevens and vice versa. Moving the Women's Rugby World Cup to 2017 will enable our players to have the opportunity to represent their country at the Olympic Games, Women's Rugby World Cup Sevens, Women's Rugby World Cup and the Women's Sevens World Series.'

On the subject of Sevens pushing out the women's Fifteens game, Carty is confident the two can co-exist. 'The two disciplines are complementary and there is a great deal of crossover at the elite level, as you will see at the Women's Rugby World Cup in France. The most important objective for us is to ensure that there is a great opportunity for our players to compete on the world's greatest stages, and we feel that we are getting there, though we must keep pressing on.

'I have no doubt that Olympic inclusion will provide a catalyst to growth, not just in Sevens but in Fifteens. It is a really exciting prospect and we are gearing up to capitalise on the feel-good factor that Olympic Games exposure will bring.'

As always England, Wales, Scotland and Northern Ireland have the same old issue. The clue is in the Team GB title. The current IOC and IRB ruling is that the highest-ranked men's and women's sides will go into the Olympics as the GB representatives. There will be no option to combine a side like the footballers achieved at London 2012.

This is reasonably straightforward in the women's game. Only the England Women are a core Sevens side and finished a creditable fourth in the 2013-14 WSWS. This achievement is made more impressive when you realise they were the highest-ranked side that weren't full-timers.

As always it's messy as to what happens next in the UK, but the men have the same issues and no one wants to miss out on a chance of going to the Olympic Games. It is, after all, the greatest show on earth.

Red Rose Champions
the Women's RWC 2014

by **SARA ORCHARD**

'As tension mounted in the Stade Jean Bouin, it was England's star Scarratt who sealed the victory. She saw a chink of daylight to cross through the Canadian defence and touch down'

After a 20-year wait, England once again got their hands on the Women's Rugby World Cup trophy. They were crowned world champions at the Stade Jean Bouin, home of Stade Français, in central Paris after a 21-9 win over Canada. After suffering three successive World Cup final defeats at the hands of New Zealand, England's victory is their second World Cup title.

England captain Katy McLean dedicated their win to the whole rugby family and the England sides who'd lost out in previous finals. The fly half and primary school teacher also hoped that the English victory would inspire more young girls to take up the sport. 'I know when I get back to school, I'm going to have everyone in my class out there playing rugby,' she said.

'There might be some reading and writing as well in between, but I think we can inspire the next generation.

'The support's been absolutely phenomenal. I've had messages during the tournament from children as young as three and five.'

The French took the tournament to their hearts and the pool matches in Marcoussis were sold out every day. National terrestrial broadcast records were broken in France as more than two million tuned in to watch.

France met Canada in the semi-finals and a 20,000-strong vociferous crowd sang out '*Allez Les Bleus*' for all in Paris to hear. However, it was the Canadians who would make their first ever World Cup final with an 18-16 win. The match included a stand-out performance from Canada wing Magali Harvey who went on to win the IRB Women's Player of the Year award.

Harvey beat off competition from her team-mate and captain Kelly Russell, France's No. 8 Safi N'Diaye and Ireland full back Niamh Briggs. IRB Chairman Bernard Lapasset said of Harvey, 'Her try against France in the semi-final was perhaps the tournament highlight and certainly one of the tries of the year. I was privileged to have been sitting in the stand to watch it live.'

The shock of the World Cup was New Zealand's failure to make it through to the semi-finals. They lost 17-14 to Ireland in their pool match after a heroic performance by the Irish side. The Black Ferns were never able to recover enough points to make the knockouts and it was the Irish who progressed to the semi-finals for the first time.

The Black Ferns head coach Brian Evans admitted other countries were

LEFT 17 August 2014. England Women's skipper Katy McLean raises aloft the Women's Rugby World Cup trophy at the Stade Jean Bouin.

always going to catch them eventually. 'The bar's been rising for the last few years, we know that, and there's a number of teams – Canada, France, obviously England and now the Irish, they're good teams. The standard is going up all the time, we prepared for that but we couldn't pull it off.'

The Irish lost 40-7 at the hands of England in the semi-finals, and the final line-up guaranteed that there would be a new name on the trophy for the first time since 1994. The Red Roses dominated the first half. Centre Emily Scarratt slotted two penalties before full back Danielle Waterman scored England's first try.

Canada's Harvey brought her team back into the match with three penalties, reducing England's lead to 11-9. As tension mounted in the Stade Jean Bouin, it was England's star Scarratt who sealed the victory. She saw a chink of daylight to cross through the Canadian defence and touch down.

England vice-captain Sarah Hunter was frank about the performance but was thrilled with the result. 'It perhaps wasn't our best performance and it didn't quite click at times, but the true team showed that, when we're under pressure, we keep going, picking each other up off the floor.

'I still can't quite believe we're world champions.'

FACING PAGE, TOP Aroha Savage of the Black Ferns is stopped by Ashleigh Baxter as Ireland defeat New Zealand in Pool B.

FACING PAGE, BOTTOM Canada's Magali Harvey receives the IRB Women's Player of the Year award from Bernard Lapasset, who in the semis had watched her run the length of the field to score against France.

BELOW England's Emily Scarratt crosses for the killer score in the final.

Summer Tours 2014
England in New Zealand

by **MICK CLEARY**

'Fleeting promise is one thing, sustained excellence quite another. England have to discover a few more gears yet, both in the forward pack as well as notably in midfield'

It is usually a forlorn task to scrabble around in the rubble of a 3-0 series defeat to find some sort of positive, to deliver a mere PR hack-job sugar-coating an uncomfortable reality. Not this time. There have been so many summer tours down below the equator that have ended in misery that the only humane thing to do was to draw a line underneath the dismal ledger of account and hope that no one ever reopened its dusty contents. But there was no need for observers to spin the truth so that it suited a particular biased end. The Kiwis did it themselves. And, no, this was no patronising wave from the world champions as the English packed their bags and headed home. 'Bad luck, you mugs, hope you get a bit closer next time.' Instead there was genuine respect for what England had brought to the trip, from the spirited uprising of the first Test, when a mix 'n' match collection had taken the All Blacks to within two minutes of ending their long sequence of victories, to a similarly late burst of defiance in Dunedin, and, let us not forget, that bristling six-try demolition job done by the midweek side over the multi-garlanded Crusaders.

Of course, there is a danger in finding too much solace in defeat. England had, after all, been taken apart in the first half of the third Test, their defence shredded by the sharp-edged New Zealand attack, killed off by their even sharper rugby brains as they spotted a weakness and exploited it to the full, running in four tries by just after the half-hour mark. It was clinical, brutal and troubling. England were a distant second-best, beaten for speed of thought and precision of execution. If they were to perform like that in their pool at the 2015 Rugby World Cup, the toughest grouping ever brought together, with high-ranking Wales and Australia ready to poop the party, then England will be left to lament exiting their hosted tournament before it really gets going in the knockout stages.

So, how to strike the balance on assessing a trip that won over many Kiwi hearts and minds but left the world order exactly as it was? Glass half-full or half-empty? Stuart Lancaster did score a notable triumph of impressing the locals but, much as the All Blacks have done for generations when coming to these parts, he would probably exchange a bit of love coming his way for more mean-spirited warriors on the

FACING PAGE Wing Marland Yarde bursts past New Zealand scrum half Aaron Smith during the third Test in Hamilton.

BELOW England's Freddie Burns takes a shot at goal in the first Test in Auckland, watched by Mike Catt and Joe Marler.

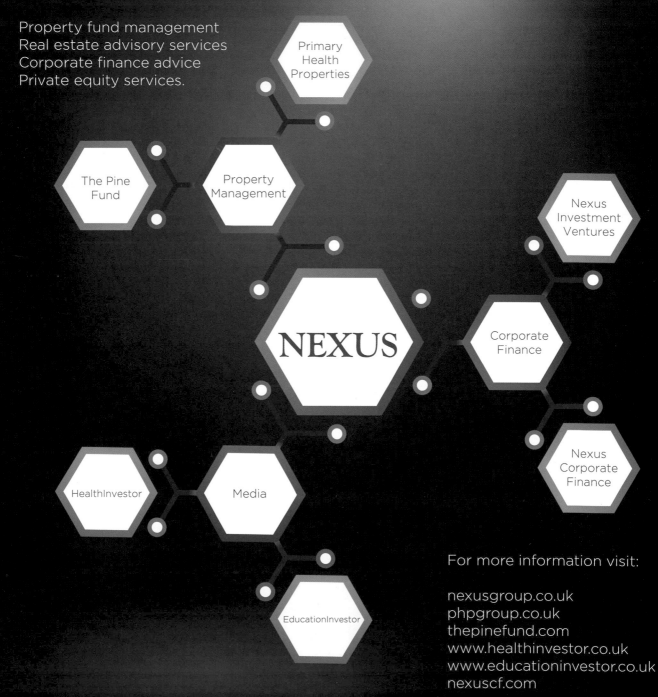

field. Lancaster's prime objective is to deliver a World Cup-challenging side by September 2015. There were times during that first-half blitzing in Hamilton when you wondered if England were any nearer their goal, particularly in midfield.

The tour schedule proved to be a serious handicap for Lancaster. The daft demands of the club-and-country season, with the Aviva Premiership final only seven days before the Test in Auckland, not only messed up his selection for that all-important first match, it effectively compromised his choices for the entire tour. To change or not to change? To reward those who went well at Eden Park, such as fly half Freddie Burns and Bath centre Kyle Eastmond, or to revert to those who had served England so well in the 2014 Six Nations Championship? Lancaster did both, and it resulted in muddle.

Eastmond, in particular, was exposed, making way for Billy Twelvetrees in Dunedin, getting the nod again at the Waikato Stadium only to be hauled off unceremoniously at half-time, a cruel end to a promising tour. Of course, England's defensive woes were not all due to Eastmond, but it will be a big call to start him again against an All Black side.

Lancaster is well aware of the dangers of false refuge. The stats do not lie, just as a scoreboard does not lie. England came to New Zealand intent on winning the series. They left without winning a Test. That is not good enough. No matter that they troubled the All Blacks for long stretches of that opening Test; that they played the more challenging, inventive rugby; that they were tough up front, with supposed back-up hooker Rob Webber proving a mighty presence, aided manfully by James Haskell and Ben Morgan. All these were plusses, but they got England nowhere.

Fleeting promise is one thing, sustained excellence quite another. England have to discover a few more gears yet, both in the forward pack as well as notably in midfield.

There were injury absentees, and the likes of Northampton prop Alex Corbisiero and Leicester back-row Tom Croft would bolster any side.

England have to solve the midfield conundrum. There is much hope invested in the arrival into union of rugby league star Sam Burgess. Even though all the vested parties are saying that Burgess

is a long-term prospect, there is little doubt that fingers are being crossed in very high places that he might adapt in super-quick time to provide the missing link for 2015. No one speaks ill of him in rugby league and even though there has been legitimate scepticism in many quarters about a rugby league player making the transition so smoothly and speedily – only Jason Robinson has managed to do so, with even Sonny Bill Williams having to serve a decent apprenticeship – the portents are good. Burgess may lack for union subtleties at the moment, but he has raw power and strength of mind, invaluable qualities at the highest level.

England did see players emerge, with Marland Yarde doing his cause no harm, albeit the odd defensive lapse also shows that there is still much to do. Nonetheless his own power, his willingness to look for work and his ability to be in the right place tell you that he will be a fixture on one of those flanks for some time to come if his form holds true. What looks equally likely is that Manu Tuilagi will not be on the other wing, or not for any extended time. Lancaster refused to admit that the decision to move him there for the second Test was a mistake even if the Leicester centre, who had played a lot of age-grade rugby in that position, did look out of sorts there. That other wing slot is still up for grabs. Chris Ashton worked his way back into contention but, like several others, looked vulnerable in that final Test.

The 2014-15 season will be a time for a final sifting of positions, with Lancaster stating quite baldly that no one's place is secure, not even his captain, Chris Robshaw. The England head coach wants to see Robshaw put under pressure for his place and took heart from the performance of Gloucester open-side Matt Kvesic against the Crusaders.

'Yes, absolutely, we want more competition at 7,' said Lancaster. 'I am unequivocal in my mind in that regard. Matt Kvesic delivered a performance against the Crusaders that I want him to bottle and become a consistent performer for Gloucester. I want him to challenge [Chris].'

The same holds true across the board.

England had promised much in the first Test, although they had to rely on the boot of Burns for their points, with Danny Cipriani chipping in with the fifth penalty to cap a promising cameo appearance from the bench. That tied the scores at 15-15, and all might have been well with England's world but for a lapse of concentration and a moment of audacity from All Black fly half Aaron Cruden, who tapped and went in the 78th minute, spurning a potentially match-winning pot at goal for an even higher reward. He eventually got it, centre Conrad Smith touching down to seal a 20-15 win for New Zealand.

England made five changes in the starting XV for the following week, seven more on the bench, as the Premiership finalists returned to the fold. England again performed with gusto in the first half, leading 10-6 at the interval thanks to a try from Yarde. And then it all went horribly wrong, the All Blacks scoring three tries in 11 minutes shortly after the restart, Ben Smith, Julian Savea and Ma'a Nonu doing the damage. England restored respectability on the scoreboard at least with late tries from Mike Brown and Ashton. The one-point margin of defeat, 28-27, was misleading.

That impression was confirmed in that third Test, Savea running amok, claiming a well-deserved hat-trick with the last play, scrum half Aaron Smith weighing in with two tries as New Zealand rounded off a fine series with a 36-13 win. It was a sobering finale although Lancaster did not believe that there would be any lasting damage to England's self-belief.

'Morale will be fine because if anything it will fire a steely determination to ensure it never happens again,' said Lancaster. 'There have been so many positives over the last 12 months that I would be very surprised if any player feels the experience has dented his self-belief to the point where he doesn't believe that he can achieve.'

Scotland All Over the World

by ALAN LORIMER

'You had to feel a tad sorry for Scotland's new coach, having to familiarise himself with a constantly changing squad while coping with an impossible tour schedule'

A dding further harsh comment to what most Scottish rugby fans judged to be the most insane tour ever conceived is like adding a grain of sand to the Sahara. It was a mad idea and whichever bureaucrat at Murrayfield dreamed up such a punishing schedule for Scotland's rugby squad deserves the welter of criticism aimed at SRU headquarters both before and after what was rightly dubbed the 'tour from hell'.

ABOVE Scotland line up after their close-run 19-17 win over Canada in Toronto – leg two of their 2014 summer tour.

Who on earth could have thought that starting a four-Test itinerary in the steamy environs of Houston, Texas, before flying north to Toronto and then taking the long haul to Argentina constituted careful planning? Admittedly the 42-strong tour selection was effectively two squads split between the first two matches and the last two, but nevertheless containing some nine players who trudged round all four Tests. If that were not bad enough, the Scotland squad were then required to play against South Africa outside the IRB Test 'window', meaning that the Scots were shorn of their England- and France-based players. To add to the ever-heightening hurdles, Scotland had to fly east from Argentina across six time zones to Port Elizabeth where they provided little more than live target practice for the Springboks. The result at the Nelson Mandela Stadium was as

inevitable as it was disheartening and did much to take the shine off the three Test wins against USA, Canada and Argentina earlier in the tour.

You had to feel a tad sorry for Scotland's new coach, Vern Cotter, having to familiarise himself with a constantly changing squad while coping with an impossible tour schedule. The Kiwi coach, having moved from the relative comfort of Clermont Auvergne, must surely have been left wondering if his decampment to Murrayfield was a wise decision. Cotter, however, will be judged on how well he prepares the Scotland squad for the World Cup and certainly not on the performances of a Scottish squad missing a number of top players recovering from injury and then weakened by the loss of the experienced Kelly Brown, Jim Hamilton and Alasdair Strokosch in addition to Duncan Taylor – all early tour casualties.

At the outset Scotland looked to have a reasonably strong side to face the USA in the heat and humidity of Houston, albeit back-row resources were stretched to the limit, resulting in a first cap for the London Irish open-side Blair Cowan. There were first Test appearances, too, for the Glasgow fly half Finn Russell and for his Scotstoun colleague Gordon Reid at loose-head. Reid was replaced by a fourth new boy in prop Alex Allan, who had played only 12 minutes of professional rugby (for Edinburgh) before winning his first cap.

Reid along with Geoff Cross ensured Scotland gave nothing away at scrum time, and with Jim Hamilton partnering Richie Gray in the second row and Johnnie Beattie at No. 8 the Scots had the better of the forward exchanges. That allowed Russell to enjoy an impressive debut that could result in the Glasgow Warrior becoming first choice at fly half for Scotland. The Scots also defended well against an aggressive Eagles side and in attack scored two scorching tries, the first by Tim Visser from a Greig Laidlaw break and the second by Stuart Hogg after showing skill in the air under the high ball. Scotland's other try was of the penalty variety from strong scrummaging, and with Laidlaw converting all three and kicking a penalty goal, the Scots emerged winners 24-6.

The Scots knew they would face a tougher task in Toronto against Canada, and if there was any complacency the 2002 Canadian win at the Thunderbird Stadium should have been a warning. Twelve years on from that victory in Vancouver, Canada came close to a repeat, only to be thwarted by a cruel refereeing decision towards the end of the match. Both sides had scored one try – Ospreys winger Jeff Hassler for Canada and lock Grant Gilchrist for Scotland – and both kickers – Canadian full back James Pritchard and Scotland scrum half Greig Laidlaw – had landed four penalty goals (Laidlaw's conversion goal was the difference between the two teams), when flanker Jebb Sinclair 'ran over' Ruaridh Jackson, leaving the Scotland replacement flat out on the turf.

The referee, suspecting an illegal challenge, consulted with the TMO and then ruled that Sinclair had led with the forearm, resulting in a red card for the flanker. Worse still for Canada the red card reversed an eminently kickable penalty signalled just seconds before the Sinclair incident and handed the Scots a get-out-of-jail pass and a chance to run down the clock to a 19-17 victory. Canada had lost but they took the plaudits for making numerous line breaks and, inspired by their Sevens exponent Phil Mack, for playing an attacking game that exposed frailties in Scotland's defence.

All the same the result made it two from two for Scotland. The win, though, was somewhat pyrrhic, especially in terms of damage to the back row. Alasdair Strokosch suffered a neck injury, Kelly Brown tore his bicep and Johnnie Beattie injured his knee, resulting in front-row replacement Kevin Bryce making his Scotland debut on the flank, and making a reasonable fist of it.

At this point the North America 'crew', which included veteran Sean Lamont, flew back to Scotland, while those players unlucky enough to be inked in for the entire tour headed south to Argentina and their final destination of Córdoba, the city forever associated in Scottish sporting folklore with the 1978 soccer World Cup and the exploits of Ally's Tartan Army. Remnants of this faithful band of followers still remain in Córdoba such was the allure of life in Argentina for several hundred from west central Scotland.

FACING PAGE Airborne Eagles skipper Todd Clever (No. 6) looks on as Scotland centre Duncan Taylor is felled by Shalom Suniula.

BELOW Lock Grant Gilchrist powers over for a score, his first for Scotland, during the opening half against Canada.

ABOVE Tomás Cubelli (No. 9) cannot stop Stuart Hogg from touching down for Scotland against the Pumas in Córdoba.

FACING PAGE Summoned from New Zealand, Adam Ashe (in scrum cap) played the full 80 minutes on debut against South Africa in Port Elizabeth.

Joining the likes of Stuart Hogg and Geoff Cross were the players assigned to the second half of the tour, together with those called up to replace a number of fallen heroes. For Cotter, it was another new beginning and undoubtedly a considerable challenge for the Kiwi boss. However, this was not too dissimilar to what was happening in the Puma camp, where a largely home-based set of players were being given the chance to test themselves at international level.

Against this new-look Puma side, Scotland, skippered by the young Edinburgh lock Grant Gilchrist, made a bright start but then succumbed to some clever handling by Argentina to trail 19-10 with ten minutes remaining; the Scots had scored a try through Hogg converted by Duncan Weir, who also landed a penalty goal. The Pumas had shown genuine attacking ability to score tries by flanker Javier Ortega Desio and replacement wing Joaquín Tuculet, their other points coming from two penalty goals and a dropped goal by fly half Nicolás Sánchez.

Scotland, however, were able to hit back, first with a Weir penalty and then with a try by scrum half Henry Pyrgos created by Tommy Seymour. Weir missed the conversion but the fly half quickly atoned with a penalty goal that gave Scotland a two points advantage. Argentina had the chance to snatch victory at the death, only for Sánchez's attempted dropped goal to sail wide of the posts, leaving the Scots 21-19 winners and, whisper it, three from three.

Touring the Americas is one thing, even if the third leg involved crossing the equator, but then to traverse the South Atlantic for a one-off game against the second strongest nation in world rugby might be considered as verging on the insane. Cotter by this time must have been wondering what on earth he was doing in South Africa in charge of a Scotland squad lacking England- and France-based players and with a pile of injuries to add to his woes. Of course because this Test match was outside the IRB window the Springboks were similarly affected, but such is the strength in depth of South Africa rugby that there is not too much difference between the top side and what might be described as an 'A' team.

In the event South Africa still had some famous names to call on – Schalk Burger on the flank, Victor Matfield at lock, Fourie du Preez at scrum half – but this was a game for a number of players likely to appear in the Springbok World Cup squad to confirm their form. Giving a mature display at fly half was the IRB Junior Player of the Year, Handré Pollard, while at centre, Jan Serfontein, who won the same title two years earlier, showed why he is ready to step into more famous boots.

Scotland with probably a tenth of the resources of South Africa were forced to make desperate selections, bringing in the uncapped Glasgow back-row Adam Ashe, who was in New Zealand on a

McPhail scholarship, and who had played only 36 minutes of rugby for his club. And without the England- and France-based players Cotter was having to rely on the resources of just two clubs, Edinburgh and Glasgow, to supply the team. In fact the Scotland side was almost a Glasgow team – and not the Scotstoun club's top selection either.

It was a predictable catastrophe. The jet-lagged and tour-weary Scotland players did everything to turn this 'Test' into an easy win for the Springboks. Scotland were out-muscled in the forward exchanges, they were second best in the contact area, they gave away penalties as though they were free marketing ploys, and against a willing Springbok back line Scotland's defence crumbled. The Scots were 19-3 down inside 15 minutes but then held their own until Tim Swinson was yellow-carded for an innocuous crime. Why do referees do this in Test matches where it is clear one side is so far on top and in which the scoreline is inconsequential? South Africa immediately took advantage, scoring from a driven line out and then adding another try before the ten-minute penalty period had expired.

In all the Boks ran in eight tries for a 55-6 win, Scotland's heaviest defeat to South Africa for 17 years and a desperate way to end a tour. It should be a warning to desk men not to put commercial considerations before the physical and psychological wellbeing of players. Whether that will be heeded remains to be seen, but there will be a number of players who will carry the scars of this 20,000-mile Odyssey for some time to come.

In defeat Pyrgos for a second successive game showed that he is ready to return to regular international rugby, Seymour confirmed his quality and flanker Rob Harley demonstrated that he can be relied upon to work for the full 80 minutes. Of the young brigade Russell, having performed well in the first two Tests, could be Scotland's answer at 10, Gilchrist has captaincy potential and Ashe, having survived the full 80 minutes, will surely add to his one cap tally.

But what the tour again exposed is Scotland's lack of depth. That has reignited calls for a third professional team and for innovative measures to deal with the sorry state of not just rugby but sport in general throughout Scotland's state schools. If the tour from hell helps in any way to address these issues, then it will be regarded in a more benign light and not as an episode in Scottish rugby history that begs to be erased from the archives.

Wales in South Africa

by GRAHAM CLUTTON

'The outstanding full back Willie le Roux released Cornal Hendricks and as the wing reached out for the corner, the Wales full back Liam Williams barged him into touch'

It would have been nigh on impossible to predict exactly what would befall the Wales squad in South Africa this summer. The Test series began with heavy defeat and improved out of all recognition before coming to a shattering conclusion in Nelspruit with Wales denied a first ever victory over the Springboks on South African soil in the most heartbreaking of circumstances.

The difficult first Test, during which the Springboks eased to victory in Durban 38-16, followed a midweek victory over an Eastern Province Kings side that were plucky but unable to live with the greater quality of a young, intuitive Welsh 'dirt-trackers' team in Port Elizabeth. Then, having been written off by all but themselves in the build-up to the second and final Test, Wales defied the odds to come within a whisker of winning. With Wales in front with less than three minutes remaining of a game that at one stage they had led 17-0, the Springboks launched one final assault along the right flank.

The outstanding full back Willie le Roux released Cornal Hendricks and as the wing reached out for the corner, the Wales full back Liam Williams barged him into touch. Referee Steve Walsh questioned the TMO about the validity of the tackle, suggesting that Williams might not have used his arms. Surely not? Surely not again? When the words filtered through to the earpiece of Walsh, the world and his wife understood the severity of the situation and held their collective breath.

LEFT A distraught Dan Biggar after a last-gasp dropped-goal attempt fails to save the second Test for Wales.

FACING PAGE Liam Williams about to make his fateful move on Cornal Hendricks as the wing goes for the line in Nelspruit.

Captain Alun Wyn Jones all but pleaded with Walsh, but his request fell on deaf ears with the official explaining that Williams' indiscretion merited a penalty try as he was the final defender. Hendricks would have scored had it not been for his illegal intervention. Morné Steyn converted from in front and that was that. A glorious victory to make rugby history became another gut-wrenching defeat.

There was no blame attached to Williams by any one of the tourists and as centre Jonathan Davies explained, the squad's level camaraderie will serve Wales well as they move towards next year's Rugby World Cup.

'I'm sure that in time he will get a bit of stick,' joked Davies. 'However, nobody was turning on Liam and asking why he did it. We are a squad, moving forward together and maybe we should never have allowed them to get into that position in the first place.

'But when we look back at the missed opportunity, it is tough. It will hurt for a very long time because we had the chance to rewrite the history books. And though we lost the game, I think many people will suggest we deserved to win it.'

The availability of Davies, amongst one or two others, for the three-match excursion had been key for coach Warren Gatland who had already been shorn of the services of captain Sam Warburton, fellow open-side Justin Tipuric, full back Leigh Halfpenny, hooker Richard Hibbard and outside half Rhys Priestland in the final weeks of the season.

Their collective absence meant a tough examination became even tougher; a genuine test of the fringe players who Gatland, to his credit, trusted in the midweek game at King's Park.

Bristol-bound Matthew Morgan, Cardiff Blues centre Cory Allen, the Scarlets utility back Jordan Williams and the Ospreys No. 8 Dan Baker were included in the party chosen in the wake of the Probables v Possibles trial game at the Liberty Stadium. Adam Jones, Gethin Jenkins and Alun Wyn

Jones were the key members of the front five, whilst Taulupe Faletau and Dan Lydiate were chosen in a back row that would see Gatland experiment with Aaron Shingler and Josh Turnbull in the absence of his first-choice open-sides. By the time the dust had settled on the tour, and Wales had returned home to gather themselves once more ahead of a season that will test them to the full, Gatland was happy that his squad was beginning to show greater strength in depth.

The trip to Eastern Kings ended in a 34-12 victory for the midweek team under Dan Lydiate – tries from Gareth Davies, James Hook, Alex Cuthbert, Allen and Turnbull paved the way for a comfortable win that saw the likes of Baker, Morgan and Jordan Williams make their mark.

Although that match and the pre-tour trial game had provided some much needed rugby for those who Gatland would pitch in to the first Test, in Durban, it was clear that the break between the end of the domestic season and the first Test had taken its toll.

Wales, who had Jamie Roberts yellow-carded after a dozen minutes, shipped a brace of tries whilst the Racing Métro centre was in the bin and trailed 28-9 at half-time as the Springboks ran riot. A Cuthbert try softened the blow, late on, but it was a comprehensive defeat that certainly upset the captain Alun Wyn Jones, who spent much of his week preaching to his players about the importance of finishing the tour on a more encouraging note.

When Wales went 17-0 up inside 22 minutes in the second Test, it was more than most could believe. Tries from Roberts and Cuthbert and seven points from the boot of Dan Biggar left the Springboks on the back foot. However, yellow cards for Biggar and the lock Luke Charteris allowed the Boks back in to the contest and by half-time the gap was just three. Still, by the time Willie le Roux responded to Ken Owens' second-half try, Wales were six points clear and within sight of the finishing line. 'We were in a great position,' said Davies. Then, disaster struck. Some said déjà vu, reflecting on the various near misses in recent years. 'You never count your chickens, but to be ahead with such a short time remaining was where we wanted to be,' added Davies.

But, as on so many previous occasions, it was not to be. 'Tough to take,' said Gatland. Still, when the upset was put to one side and the management began to reflect on a series that did at least answer one or two questions, there were more smiles than grimaces.

Davies said, 'In the Six Nations you are together for about eight weeks and everything becomes automatic and you understand what everyone is doing. We did not have a lot of preparation time before we left and it probably showed in the first Test.

'If you look back at Australia in 2012, the first week we were way off the pace, the second week we should have won and the third week we were competing again for victory. The more time the squad spends together the better we get because there is more familiarity among us.'

Gatland said, 'We have got an incredibly tough pool for the World Cup, but we can look forward to it with some confidence.

'We know on the day if we get the bounce of the ball and a couple of things go our way we are good enough to compete with the top teams in the world.

'We are probably a little bit off New Zealand at the moment, but we have demonstrated with South Africa and Australia in the last couple of years it's just a case of getting over the line.

'It's about making sure that you get that elusive victory over a southern hemisphere team and then mentally that changes that whole focus.

'They responded brilliantly between the Tests. We purposefully came over to put ourselves under pressure, with some replication of World Cup preparation. It meant we could go away and debate potential scenarios in terms of the way we do handle the short turnaround for World Cup games.

'We knew in that first week that the Test team didn't have a lot of time together, but we were able to have a lot more time together between the matches and the guys responded incredibly well. As a coaching team we are proud. At the end of the hard season, they could have capitulated. They didn't do that. This group of players took their opportunity, as proud Welshmen who were proud to put that jersey on.'

The emergence of Samson Lee, Turnbull, Baker, Morgan and Allen, in particular, will be key as Wales begin to count down to the World Cup. For Gatland, it was a tour of genuine importance – however bitter the pill.

Private Banking | Wealth Planning | Investment Management

ARBUTHNOT LATHAM
Private Bankers
Since 1833

For business.
For family.
For life.

Wealth is made of much more than money. It is realising hopes and dreams, passions and partnerships. At Arbuthnot Latham we strive to see beyond the obvious to help people achieve what really matters.

t: 020 7012 2500   arbuthnotlatham.co.uk

Ireland in Argentina

by PETER O'REILLY

'On the other hand, defence coach Les Kiss was surely seething that they conceded two tries both weeks, having been so mean during the Six Nations'

Ireland scored their first Test victory in Argentina, recorded their first Test series win in the southern hemisphere since 1979 and Joe Schmidt blooded five new caps – not the worst return from a two-week tour to Argentina, surely? Yet after both Tests, in Resistencia and Tucumán, it was the Argentinians who wore broad smiles as they conducted mini laps of honour.

The Pumas were missing 13 of their front-liners so had gone into the series as underdogs, largely a collection of home-based amateurs taking on the reigning Six Nations champions. That they reduced the losing margin – from 12 points in Resistencia (29-17) to six in Tucumán (23-17) – strengthened the sense that they had derived more developmental value than the visitors. The Pumas' feel-good factor was enhanced by scoring late tries two weeks running.

Schmidt tried to maintain the sunny demeanour of a coach who has now won six of his last seven Tests, but even before departure it had been obvious that this wasn't his idea of The Ideal Tour, coming as it did 15 months from the Rugby World Cup.

No matter where Ireland toured, their preparation would have been compromised by having Leinster, Ulster and Munster all involved in the knockout stages of the PRO12 – as it turned out, Schmidt only spent a day and a half with his players between winning the Six Nations and boarding the plane for Buenos Aires.

BELOW Ian Madigan, who scored in the game, breaks the tackle of Matías Orlando during the second Test between Argentina and Ireland at Tucumán.

While the tour afforded him an uninterrupted fortnight with the players, the schedule didn't make things particularly easy. In their wisdom, the Argentine Rugby Union scheduled the Tests for far-flung corners of the country, which ensured a fair degree of travel, even on such a short tour. As it turned out, Schmidt only had four proper field training sessions in two weeks, at a time when he was trying to involve 29 players.

As a result, he tried to cram as much work into every field session and every meeting as possible. This was no sightseeing trip, and Jamie Heaslip, for one, bemoaned the fact that this had been a tour of hotel rooms, departure lounges and training venues – although there was a visit to the Hurling Club in Buenos Aires. Such is the lot of the international rugby player.

Because the Pumas wouldn't be at full strength, Schmidt was able to leave first-choice players like Sean O'Brien, Cian Healy and Tommy Bowe at home to rehab various physical niggles so that they could start the season fresh. But he could have done without losing Robbie Henshaw and Marty Moore on the eve of departure.

For Schmidt, one of the main purposes of the tour was to develop depth at two of his problem positions – tight-head prop and especially outside centre, given Brian O'Driscoll's recent retirement. Henshaw had been virtually guaranteed to start both Tests at 13 so his withdrawal with a finger injury was a major blow. Meanwhile, it had been hoped that Moore would continue to pile pressure on veteran Mike Ross, but he too had to withdraw.

As it turned out, the main winners of the tour play in positions where Schmidt already has reasonable depth. Simon Zebo went from being a marginal player to starting both Tests and doing well in both, especially the second, when he underlined his attacking edge with a great try but also worked hard and effectively in defence – one of his weaknesses.

Robbie Diack and Rhys Ruddock took turns to wear Peter O'Mahony's No. 6 jersey, and both did so with distinction. Diack's line-out work in the first Test was particularly impressive – though the line out was an area of strength in general, as Rory Best had 100 per cent accuracy with his darts over the course of two weeks. Meanwhile Ruddock's ball-carrying in Tucumán was outstanding.

Ireland's set-pieces were generally excellent, and while this is a group skill, Jack McGrath made a big impression, both as a starter in the first Test and coming off the bench in the second. Schmidt can also be happy that he has attacking threats at fly half, given that Johnny Sexton scored yet another try and Ian Madigan finished with typical style to put Ireland out of danger in Tucumán.

On the other hand, defence coach Les Kiss was surely seething that they conceded two tries both weeks, having been so mean during the Six Nations. Partly it was down to the brilliant evasion skills of the Pumas, but mainly it was the lack of cohesion in midfield, where the absence of O'Driscoll and Gordon D'Arcy was keenly felt. Darren Cave was tried at outside centre and inside, with Fergus McFadden having a run at 13 in Tucumán. Nothing really worked, in attack or defence.

Meanwhile at tight-head, Rodney Ah You's 13-minute performance off the bench in Resistencia wasn't strong enough to earn him a second shot – in fact, McGrath was chosen as tight-head back-up for week two, which confirmed the Ah You experiment as a failure.

'I've learned a little bit about some players I didn't know much about,' said Schmidt. 'And the players have learned. I think a few of them are a little bit shell-shocked at what the level is and sometimes when you have had that shock you get the head down and you work a bit harder because you know that you are going to have to be a little bit better prepared next time. These were disappointing performances in patches, but if that's the outcome, then I'd be pretty happy.'

Ireland captain Paul O'Connell was determined to take positives from the venture, even though he conceded it had been far from perfect.

'I'm not disappointed with the tour,' O'Connell said. 'I think two weeks working with Joe is, for me anyway, an incredible learning experience and I've really enjoyed the tour. I do wish we'd been a bit more aggressive with one another, driven standards a little bit more. That's what good teams do, that's what tight teams do.

'It's a little bit of getting to know one another over the past two weeks and that probably showed a little bit on the pitch. For everyone on this tour it's a big, big learning curve; even for a lot of the guys who playcd in the Six Nations. It's exciting being in Ireland camp. So, while the results and performances have been disappointing, I think there's been a bit of learning done.'

FACING PAGE Flanker Robbie Diack soars above the Pumas to win line-out ball for Ireland in Resistencia.

BELOW Rhys Ruddock, who wore the No. 6 shirt in the second Test, takes the direct route in Tucumán.

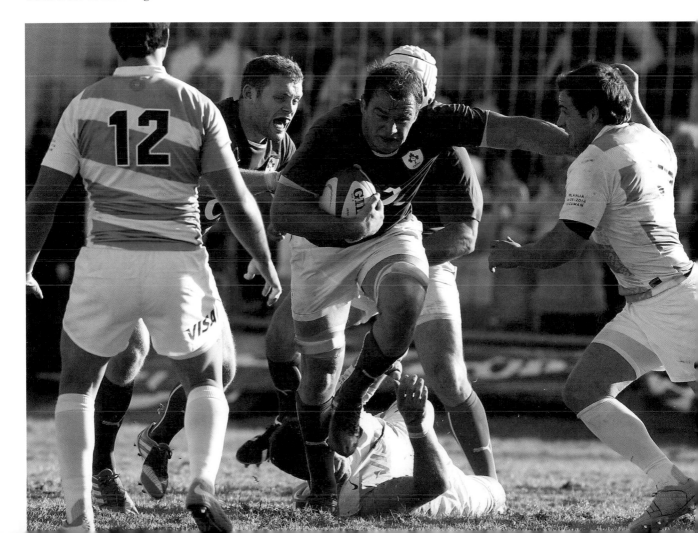

LOCH FYNE®
SEAFOOD & GRILL

"We started life as a small shack selling oysters on Scotland's West Highland route at the head of Loch Fyne. Our fish is sustainably sourced, either from abundant wild stocks or responsibly farmed"

- Rated No.1 for "Customer Satisfaction" and again for "Food Quality" in the Peach Brand Track consumer survey

- 41 restaurants nationwide, most of which are in unique historic or listed buildings

- A la carte menu with a wide range of fresh seafood and fish including our famous oysters and platters plus meat and vegetarian options

- Daytime set menu of 2 or 3 courses each with a complimentary side from £10.45

- Range of quality wines by the glass or bottle, selected by our Master wine buyer to complement our dishes

- Fresh fish and seafood available from our cold counter for you to purchase to cook at home

to find your local restaurant, view our menus or book a table, visit
www.lochfyneseafoodandgrill.co.uk

HOME FRONT

Turbulent Times
the State of Rugby in Wales
by STEVE BALE

'Somehow the regions have since done enough to foster three Welsh Grand Slams and the near miss of the 2011 World Cup semi-final, lost – familiarly by a point – to France in Auckland'

The condition of Welsh rugby caters for an endless debate, at once infuriating, illogical and a thing of wonder considering this is a small country which on numbers alone should not be capable of creating a team who can run South Africa as close as they did in the summer.

At a time of unprecedented turbulence in the game in the Principality – with the four regional sides who give Welsh players their daily bread forever at loggerheads with their own Welsh Rugby Union – here was something to calm everyone down, and not before time.

But the truly fascinating thing about the excruciating 31-30 defeat by the Springboks in Nelspruit was that it was not greeted with the relief of former years but with bitter frustration that yet again Wales had missed an opportunity they had been comfortably good enough to create.

Those of us who go back to a more golden time – yes, the Seventies – know that as well as routinely completing Triple Crowns and as often as not winning the Five Nations with a Grand Slam, the Welsh never extended that golden touch to fingering the All Blacks.

Apartheid South Africa was not part of polite rugby society. Australia were not what they soon became. So the real, in a way only, yardstick for Wales being as good as most Welsh people imagined was New Zealand. And it never happened.

Since then we have been so traumatised by the barren years that the turnaround in Welsh fortunes over the past decade has been a marvel. From the nadir of the 96-13 1998 defeat in Pretoria to a single-pointer in 2014. It has, as they say these days, been a journey.

But where does it leave Welsh rugby? The evidence of the game's contraction at its grass roots may be a consequence of the economic background but, even with the most favourable reading, is inevitably also evidence of the WRU's failure to stem the decline.

This lay behind the Extraordinary General Meeting in Port Talbot last June where the union gained a majority of quasi-North Korean proportions at 97 per cent in defeating a motion of no confidence in its stewardship by 462 votes to four with 18 abstentions.

It did come with a promise to 'listen', implying that they had not been doing so sufficiently though mea culpas in the shambles of the union's relationship with the Ospreys, Scarlets, Blues and Dragons have been hard to find.

The regions threw in their lot with the English Premiership when the row over the future of European sub-international competition was at its fiercest, and won. The Premiership, and by extension the regions, now drive the successor to the Heineken Cup.

In fact there was a serious, though never verified, suggestion that in Swansea, Llanelli, Cardiff and Newport it would not have been

FACING PAGE Ken Owens, a try scorer in the match, brings down Cornal Hendricks, another key figure in the game, as Wales run the Springboks desperately close in Nelspruit.

BELOW Despair for Wales as they go down 9-8 to France in Auckland in the semi-finals of RWC 2011.

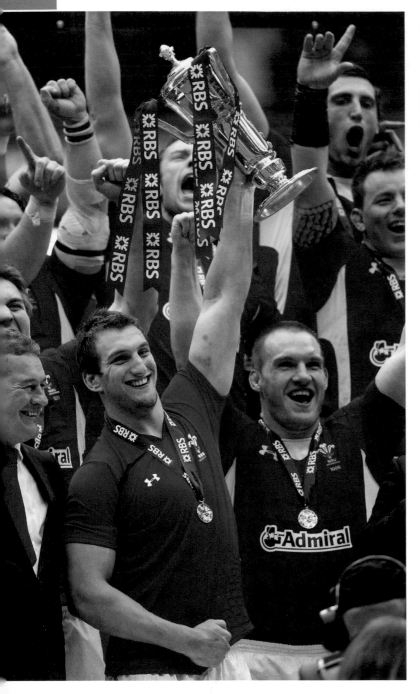

regarded as a total calamity if the protracted Euro-argument had ended in failure and led to a proper Anglo-Welsh league.

Here the rationale is that the PRO12 – to which, in the absence of any alternative, the regions are reluctantly committed – provided them not only with inadequate 'domestic' competition but also, and more especially, a season-long list of unattractive fixtures.

Receiving Italian and Scottish opposition at unpopular kick-off times, or even the Irish provinces for that matter, was not calculated to pull in punters in the numbers that would have made the regional game more meaningful. Now imagine if it were Leicester, Saracens or Harlequins.

Regional identity – no problem for Cardiff Blues and the Scarlets of Llanelli; miraculously forged by the Ospreys of Swansea-Neath; most difficult of all for the Dragons of Newport-Gwent – has been an issue from the moment the great club rivalries were subverted by the union in 2003. Somehow the regions have since done enough to foster three Welsh Grand Slams and the near miss of the 2011 World Cup semi-final, lost – familiarly by a point – to France in Auckland. The French then lost the final to New Zealand, by a point.

An alternative analysis, not unwelcome in official circles, is that under the coaching of Warren Gatland the Wales team have in effect become the fifth region by taking the players out of their own regions for such long periods that they spend as much time nationally as they do locally.

If so, it has undeniably been a success, particularly by comparison with the dire decades of the Eighties and Nineties. But when it came to those leading players with contracts to renew, with the WRU dangling central contracts like an angler at a salmon farm, what did they do?

By the end of last season, when contracts were up, Wales captain Sam Warburton was the only one to have taken the bait. Leigh Halfpenny and Jonathan Davies were already off to France. Alun Wyn Jones and Rhys Priestland set a different example by staying in Swansea and Llanelli respectively.

There were others as well. This would hardly matter if the union had not been so committed to taking central control. At the Six Nations launch in London last January, one Wales functionary was postulating Warburton could be only one of as many as two dozen. It never happened.

As the nonpareil Gerald Davies, a board member, told the extraordinary meeting, the Welsh Rugby Union did not have a good image. Perhaps, in fact certainly, that transmitted itself to senior players. Priestland himself had said the union/region stand-off was 'doing my head in'.

Yet despite everything, despite a background that would surely impact on performance if they so allowed, Wales could go to South Africa and get as close in their second Test as England did in their second in New Zealand. What if, behind the scenes, all was sweetness and light? If only.

In that second Test in Nelspruit, Wales showed moral fibre as well as power and panache to recover from the 38-16 drubbing they had taken a week earlier in Durban. The closest they had ever previously been in South Africa was a 19-8 defeat in Cape Town in 2002.

They lost in Nelspruit to Morné Steyn's conversion of a penalty try awarded for a mindless no-arms tackle on the try line by Liam Williams on Cornal Hendricks. There are some who thought Hendricks had lost the ball before the illicit impact, but as Gatland had no complaint, any alternative view is irrelevant.

The underlying point is that even after a modest 2014 Six Nations Wales are as close, still, as they have ever been. Gatland has developed a team with the muscularity to complement the immemorial innate skill of the dashing and devious Welshman of rugby stereotype. There again, Wales were this close three years ago at the global gathering in New Zealand. If that means they have actually stood still, next year's World Cup pool shared with England and Australia remains as threatening for them now as it was when the draw was made almost a year ago.

Despair to Ecstasy
London Welsh Turn It Around

by **NEALE HARVEY**

'But the real reason for London Welsh's success was an overwhelming refusal to buckle and die that was rooted in the aftermath of that defeat to Northampton'

Picture the scene. It's 14 April 2013 at a rapidly emptying Kassam Stadium in Oxford. London Welsh have just lost 31-14 to Northampton and been relegated from the Aviva Premiership. Their main benefactor, Kelvin Bryon, has recently announced in the media that he is walking away, an exodus of coaches and players is about to start and rumours over the club's future have already begun. The Premiership dream has died and been replaced by a grim fight for survival.

Seventeen months on, the picture could not be more different. Bryon is back, his busy chequebook whirring, the Exiles are still in Oxford, and under the button-bright, enthusiastic leadership of head coach Justin Burnell, they are now embarking on another Aviva Premiership campaign after overcoming seemingly insuperable odds to win last season's Greene King IPA Championship. As resurgences go, it's on a par with England recovering to win cricket's 1981 Ashes.

Home and away victories over Bristol in the Championship final provided London Welsh's passage back to the top flight. But the real reason for their success was an overwhelming refusal to buckle and die that was rooted in the aftermath of that defeat to Northampton.

Bleddyn Phillips, the Exiles chairman, explains, 'You don't throw the towel in and say, "game over". The test of a good, resilient club is to overcome adversity and respond positively. Players and coaches departed, but we rebuilt quickly and bringing in Justin Burnell as head coach and promoting Gordon Ross to assistant coach was very important. We lost players, but 40 per cent of the squad eventually stayed, plus we brought in some very good players too. We believed we had a good, competitive squad. What we didn't realise was just how good it could be.'

Phillips' real masterstroke, though, was persuading Bryon to reverse his decision to walk away. He said, 'London Welsh is in Kelvin's blood and vice versa. To try and separate the two is very hard and with the way things turned around, the feel-good factor within the team and the renewed sense of purpose we had, I hoped that generated a degree of encouragement for Kelvin to say, "Yes, I'm still in the game," and "Yes, this is a club still worth spending time and money on." Keeping Kelvin on board was crucial and we like to think he's been rewarded for his commitment.'

Having had one stab at cracking the Oxford market – and to a degree succeeding, as regular crowds of 5000 and a bumper Christmas gate of over 10,000 against London Wasps proved – Welsh are determined to make an even better fist of their second stint in the Aviva Premiership. Accordingly, the club has recruited a locally based chief executive, Mike Stevens, and relocated its offices and full-time community operation to Oxford. Stevens, who previously worked as commercial manager at Leicester Tigers, believes the enhanced local connection will pay big dividends.

He explained, 'A key part of what we did at Tigers was working with the local community – business, clubs, schools and universities – and I have no intention of reinventing the wheel. What worked for Leicester can work for London Welsh. Two years ago, we played Wasps and there was a near capacity crowd at the Kassam, so we know it's possible. We've just got to look at the whole product, engage the Oxfordshire community and provide a good match-day experience.'

Having committed London Welsh to staying in Oxford for at least three more years, Phillips knows it is make or break as far as providing sustainable top-flight rugby in the area is concerned. 'It's important to recognise that we're committed to Oxford and the fact we attracted a crowd of 5000 for our Championship final match against Bristol on a wet Wednesday night proves there is very good support for London Welsh. It cannot be done overnight, but if we can build on that support in the Premiership it would be tremendous for our longer-term prospects here.'

RIGHT The Kassam Stadium, 'Home of the London Welsh', falls silent ahead of the match against Bristol on Remembrance Sunday 2013.

BELOW New Exiles signing Olly Barkley attacks for Grenoble against Wasps during the Amlin Challenge Cup clash at Adams Park in December 2013.

As ever, performances on the pitch will help immeasurably, and following promotion Burnell wasted no time strengthening his squad, with one of the headline signings being that of former Bath, Gloucester and England fly half Olly Barkley. Burnell, who retained the majority of last season's character-fuelled side and will have a squad of 50-plus players at his disposal, said, 'I've not brought in people with their own agendas, I've strengthened with people who have the London Welsh mindset, which means they'll work hard for their team-mates and the supporters.'

Burnell, an abrasive former flank forward who previously coached the Cardiff Blues, left Wales to broaden his horizons after feeling unappreciated in his home country. And he has relished the opportunity afforded him in England, saying, 'London Welsh offered me an ideal chance to get back into sharp-end coaching. I had nine

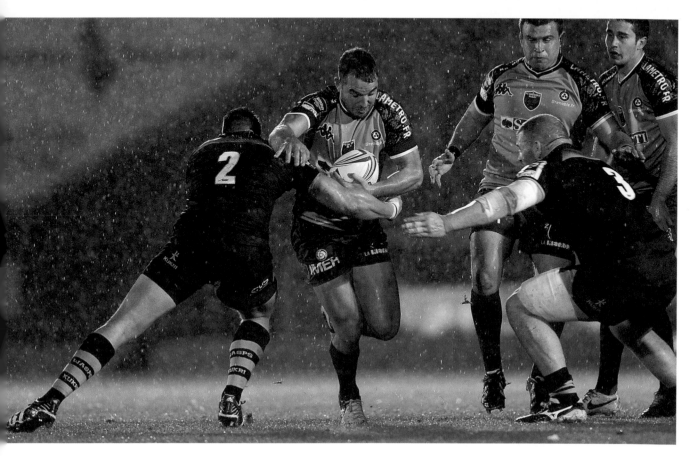

good years at Cardiff, coming right through their coaching system from the academy to the top job, but it finished abruptly and that was that.

'It's not been a case of coming here to prove any points. I felt when I was with the Blues I did a good job and I learnt a lot from working with Dai Young, who's now at Wasps, but what quite easily gets forgotten in Wales is that they can be quite dismissive of their own. Welsh rugby must be doing something right when you see what guys like Rob Howley and Neil Jenkins have done with Wales and the Lions, but the Welsh Rugby Union could do more for its own people.'

In his heart of hearts, Burnell did not expect to lead the Exiles to promotion in his first year. 'What did I expect? I just wanted stability, to come in and work with Kelvin and Bleddyn and just try to get a system and structure in place so London Welsh could maintain their position and move forward. I honestly didn't realise quite how quickly we could gel and how the squad would grow. But promotion was deserved. We were on that final furlong behind Bristol, the little red horse coming on the inside ... on the fence, on the fence, then crossing the line first at the death.'

Having scaled the heights, can Welsh stay in the Premiership this time? Burnell concedes, 'The Premiership's powerful and we're under no illusions or stupid mindsets. Last season we wanted to get into the top four of the Championship and maintain stability, but we exceeded that. My focus now, and that of my squad and management, will purely be on staying in the Premiership ... nothing more, nothing less, no magical dreams or any of that. When you're playing against the likes of Northampton and Saracens, our total focus will simply be on being able to compete.'

Phillips believes, though. 'We can survive,' he insists. 'We certainly gave it a good crack last time and we learnt some lessons along the way. We won more points in our year in the Premiership than Worcester or Newcastle did last season, so it shows we can be competitive. People wrote us off before but we won five games and could have won seven or eight, so as most of our squad is still with us and we've significantly added to it, I think we're in very good shape.

'It's a very exciting period in London Welsh's history and we're looking forward to it hugely. We hope to do ourselves proud and the Premiership proud as well. We're definitely up for the challenge and it wouldn't be fair to our players, coaches or supporters if we weren't.'

That little red horse may have some legs in it yet.

To the Very End
the 2013-14 Aviva Premiership
by CHRIS HEWETT

'Northampton just about saw off their nearest and not-so-dearest from Leicester in the race for a home semi-final, only to find themselves up against … yes, you guessed it'

When a 135-game Aviva Premiership campaign played out over nine months in all winds and weathers is decided by one last close-range plunge for the line in the final seconds of the concluding period of extra time before a rapt full-house audience at Twickenham, it is reasonable to suppose that English club rugby is doing something right. This was not a thought that crossed the minds of the Northampton players as they awaited a ruling on the legitimacy of Alex Waller's title-winning try from the so-called 'video ref' – if truth be told, they were too tired to think of anything other than their own exhaustion – but during the days of reflection that followed the most gripping denouement in the history of the tournament, there was common agreement that this had been a special season.

Special for the right reasons – the positive reasons – rather than the negative ones. Just for once, the public conversation was driven by events at the top of the table rather than the bottom: Worcester, armed with a resourceful new rugby director in Dean Ryan and a couple of admirably consistent performers in the full back Chris Pennell and the back-row forward Jonathan Thomas

but utterly bereft in most other respects, hit rock bottom early in the piece and stayed there for the duration. By mid-spring, there was no serious discussion over the identity of the relegation fall guys. The Midlanders knew they were stuffed, and so did everyone else.

On the sunnier side of the street there was no such clarity. Northampton and Saracens started strongly, held things together through the upheaval of the autumn Test programme and the destabilising spread of the Six Nations Championship, and duly ended up in the final – although the eventual champions had the odd funny five minutes between the back end of March and the middle of April, which coincided, strangely enough, with the return of George North, Luther Burrell, Lee Dickson, Dylan Hartley, Courtney Lawes and Tom Wood from international duty. But this was far from the whole story.

Beneath them the sands shifted from one round of matches to the next and made a mockery of the pre-tournament talk of a 'two-tier league': Northampton, Saracens and the perennial contenders Leicester in an elite group, protected from the hoi polloi by their vast strength in depth; everyone else in another group, making do and mending to the best of their limited ability. Bath, Harlequins and Sale were anything but second-class citizens and there were times when Exeter fancied their chances of mounting a challenge for a play-off place, although they fell away sharply after winning the LV= Cup and celebrating their first major trophy with the appropriate degree of enthusiasm. (A

ABOVE Worcester Warriors full back Chris Pennell puts boot to ball against London Irish at Sixways.

FACING PAGE Skipper Tom Wood is jubilant as he scores a late, late try to put 14-man Saints in the final at the expense of Leicester Tigers. Northampton had lost prop Salesi Ma'afu to a 57th-minute red card for thumping Tom Youngs.

week later, as they were leaking the best part of 50 points at Welford Road, it was tempting to wonder whether the Devonian hangover was literal as well as metaphorical.)

Bath, lavishly resourced by the ambitious Bruce Craig, were very much a work in progress: Mike Ford, the former England defence coach, was now top dog – for the avoidance of doubt, the rugby director Gary Gold was out of a job by Christmas – and there were one or two disappointing performances in the opening weeks of the campaign. Not least at Saracens, where Ford and his fellow think-tankers were too clever by half in their team selection and paid the price. But with the coach's son George taking advantage of his first-choice status at outside half and another new recruit, the unusually substantial Matt Garvey, offering something approaching complete reliability on the blind-side flank, they quickly started stringing results together, particularly at home on the banks of the Avon.

A similar story unfolded at Sale, although the northerners could hardly be described as a mirror image of the richer, swankier West Countrymen. Another widely discussed member of the No. 10 fraternity, Danny Cipriani, rediscovered the best of himself after deciding he was tired of everyone thinking the worst of him and there were striking contributions from a couple of New Zealanders, the flanker Daniel Braid and the lock Michael Paterson. The latter, English qualified, had joined from Cardiff Blues in the summer of 2013. By the following summer, he was a Red Rose tourist in his own land – just reward for a debut Premiership campaign of startling consistency.

If Harlequins were less of a surprise package – they had, after all, won the title in 2012 – their resilience in the face of an injury list from hell ran every bit as deep as Leicester's and was equally worthy of respect. There were times when the Londoners barely had a functioning front row or a viable locking partnership or a half-decent centre combination to their name, yet they continually found ways of staring adversity in the face and forcing it to blink first. Could anyone have imagined that the journeyman hooker Dave Ward or the young tight-head prop Kyle Sinckler would make such a significant impact on events? Nostradamus himself would have hedged his bets.

Between the four sides chasing Saints and Saracens, there were some pulsating contests. Sale's late-season victory under the lights at Bath was a thing of ugly beauty, if that makes sense; Quins' home win over Leicester, another Friday night extravaganza, generated more heat than an industrial furnace. Not until the final weekend of round-robin fixtures did the make-up of the knockout stage become clear, Quins beating Bath at the Stoop with a performance rich in pride and passion.

While all this was unfolding before paying customers from Newcastle in the northeast to Exeter in the southwest, those paid to ensure that the union game remains fit for public consumption were fighting battles of their own. There were two principal areas of dispute: an interminable debate over the future of cross-border European competitions, which proved more effective than nerve gas in sending rugby folk to sleep, and the argument over the increasing use of television technology, which generally had the opposite effect on the oval-ball masses.

While the referees themselves were concluding that too much telly is bad for you – by the end of the season, many of the most senior officials in England were admitting, albeit in a whisper, that the sport was placing itself at serious risk by following cricket into George Orwell territory – they did not feel sufficiently confident to trust their own eyes rather than turn to the all-seeing eye in the sky. Constant referrals 'upstairs' had a distorting effect on some of the season's most compelling matches, including the final. A final that deserved better.

Northampton just about saw off their nearest and not-so-dearest from Leicester in the race for a home semi-final, only to find

FACING PAGE Bath fly half George Ford leaves Quins' Mike Brown sprawling as he runs away to score at the Stoop. The England full back, also a try scorer, had the last laugh as the London side won 19-16 on the last weekend of the regular season.

BELOW Sale flanker Daniel Braid tries to get hold of Wasps' Andy Goode as the Sharks win 21-17 at Adams Park.

themselves up against … yes, you guessed it. The reigning champions travelled down the M1 to Franklin's Gardens in full warpaint, and for much of the contest, which had a strong whiff of 'stone-cold classic' about it straight from the kick-off, they seemed the likelier winners. But the likes of Lawes and Wood are ferocious competitors these days and it was the latter, captain in the absence of the injured Hartley, who broke the Tigers in the closing seconds with a never-to-be-forgotten try in the left corner.

So it was that the Saints headed for their Twickenham date with Saracens, who had enjoyed a far easier time of it in their own semi-final – Harlequins were not at their most persuasive that day, to say the least – but had since suffered the excruciating pain of Heineken Cup final defeat at the hands of Toulon. For their part, Northampton had won the second-tier Amlin Challenge Cup by beating Bath and had been granted an additional day's rest by the calendar. All things considered, they were in a better frame of mind, not to mention a better state of physical health, ahead of the title showdown.

Yet Saracens were the more driven in the emotional sense, largely because their captain, Steve Borthwick, would be retiring at close of play. Borthwick had been a model professional, although it is not always the case that model professionals are treated with due respect by those denied the privilege of working alongside them. The Cumbrian was a victim of this disconnect: wholly misunderstood by many of his fiercest critics, he was held in undying regard by the vast majority of those he led.

Even though he was playing injured – the 34-year-old lock had ripped a pectoral muscle during the Quins semi-final – there was something implacable about his performance against Northampton. Implacable, but ultimately fruitless, although Saracens might have won a tourniquet-tight game in normal time had Owen Farrell, the England outside half, not kicked the ball high into the Twickenham heavens in celebration after scoring a second-half try and done himself a mischief as a consequence. (It was during a long period of treatment in the in-goal area that the television match official – yes, him again – spotted a forward pass in the build-up and wiped the points from the record. 'I won't be doing that again,' muttered Farrell subsequently.)

In the event, it was the unheralded Waller who decided matters from the traditional front-rower's distance of no distance at all. In a Premiership of fine margins, it was the only ending that could have made sense.

Arrival of the Chiefs
the 2013-14 LV= Cup

by PAUL BOLTON

'The competition was once more played on international weekends which meant that clubs again used the cup to give first-team exposure to some of their talented youngsters'

Exeter's remarkable rise to national prominence continued as they won their first major trophy in their 143-year history with a 15-8 win over Northampton at their own Sandy Park headquarters. In previous seasons, winning the Anglo-Welsh Cup would have secured Exeter a place in the following season's Heineken Cup, but that was taken away in the protracted discussions that led to the formation of the new European Rugby Champions Cup.

Instead Exeter had to settle for an open-top bus parade around the city, which gave their fanatical supporters, many of whom had roared them to success over Northampton, another chance to celebrate the cup win.

The decision to stage the final at Sandy Park rather than Worcester proved an inspired one, although the organisers dropped lucky with Exeter's progress, which ensured a sell-out crowd. Exeter's win halted Northampton's 13-match unbeaten run, but it was also to be tinged with sadness as it proved to be the last appearance for their hooker Chris Whitehead.

Whitehead, 27, who joined Exeter from Wasps ahead of their first Premiership season in 2010, scored the opening try in the final from a driving maul but suffered a neck injury during the match and announced his retirement a week later.

Exeter's other try in the final fittingly was scored by Dean Mumm, their captain and former Australia lock, who rounded off a superb passing move. 'I haven't been at this club for a long time but it's a very proud area of England in terms of its rugby prowess and this club has a very proud history,' Mumm said.

'It's a great moment, our first piece of silverware in the top league. Throughout the second half I thought our defence was outstanding.

'We were under quite a bit of pressure territorially, as well as they had a lot of possession. We stood up strong.'

Exeter's cup win compensated for a moderate Premiership campaign in which they missed out on qualification for the new top-flight European competition. It also enhanced the reputation of their head coach Rob Baxter, previously an inspirational captain at the club. 'What is pleasing for me is seeing the players rewarded for their hard work this season,' Baxter said.

'We did a lot of what we said we were going to do. I thought our forwards really fronted up and that kept a lot of pressure off us in a lot of ways.

'We dealt with Northampton's very good maul, stood in front of them at scrum time and that kept us in the game.

'The conditions were perfect for us – this is the Chiefs' time of year as I keep telling people – and we are proving that is the case.

ABOVE Exeter skipper, former Wallaby lock Dean Mumm, touches down in the 49th minute for his side's second try.

FACING PAGE Chris Whitehead signs a Chiefs fan's drum during the club's open-air bus parade through Exeter. The Chiefs hooker scored a try in the final at Sandy Park before a neck injury ended his match – and led to his retirement from rugby a week later.

'I want them to get used to it because playing big games at this time of year is what it is all about. It was a big game at our ground, we had a lot of support here and they're rewarded, just like the players.'

Northampton's disappointment at another final defeat was to be short-lived as they beat Bath to win the Amlin Challenge Cup at Cardiff Arms Park, then Saracens to lift the Aviva Premiership title for the first time in a nerve-shredding finale at Twickenham.

Northampton paid for a sluggish first half at Exeter and their fightback, led by lock Samu Manoa's 70th-minute try, was repelled. 'We talked about getting a good start and we had a poor start,' said Northampton director of rugby Jim Mallinder.

'We dropped the ball and they scored from the driven line out, so we went behind. We did get a bit of pressure then and what you want to do is score from that and take your opportunities. We didn't.

'I remember a five-metre scrum on their line. We had a line out close to their line as well and just couldn't get over. So that made it a little bit uphill.'

Exeter's successful cup campaign began with a 19-5 home win over Harlequins, the defending champions, at Sandy Park in November, but they then slipped to a 37-15 defeat at Bath in their second match. Successive wins over the Ospreys and Worcester in the New Year revived their semi-final ambitions, but only after Sale had slipped to a surprise 37-36 defeat against the Ospreys at Bridgend Ford Brewery Field. Sale led 28-13 then 36-20, but Sam Davies converted Aisea Natoga's hat-trick try from the final play of the match to clinch a dramatic win for the Ospreys.

In the semi-finals, Exeter avenged their earlier defeat at the Recreation Ground, with two tries from full back Luke Arscott and another from replacement wing Fetu'u Vainikolo clinching a 22-19 victory and their first win over Bath since 1978.

Northampton easily wrapped up Pool Four with four straight wins including a 20-16 victory against Saracens at Franklin's Gardens which secured a rematch in the semi-finals. England full back Ben Foden returned to action after three months on the sidelines with a knee injury and helped Northampton to a 26-7 win.

The final was the fifth successive all-English affair in another lean season for the four Welsh regions. There were just six wins for the Welsh sides, including Scarlets' 21-13 home victory over

Newport Gwent Dragons at the Parc y Scarlets in the opening round and Cardiff Blues' 21-13 success at the Ospreys the following week. But Scarlets were then trounced 51-10 by Saracens on the rubber-crumb surface at Allianz Park, the season's heaviest defeat in the competition.

Harlequins' home pool match against Leicester was abandoned on safety grounds after 71 minutes after a tornado hit the Stoop, dislodging scaffolding and blowing advertising hoardings and debris across the pitch. As more than 60 minutes had been played, the result – a 20-6 win to Harlequins – stood but the abandonment denied both sides the opportunity of a bonus point. Leicester's 35-17 home defeat against Bath the following week extinguished their semi-final hopes.

The competition was once more played on international weekends which meant that clubs again used the cup to give first-team exposure to some of their talented youngsters. Northampton blooded two sons of former Saints in fly half Sam Olver, son of the former England hooker John, and Howard Packman, whose father Frank played 376 games for the club as a centre/wing.

Gloucester threw Ollie Thorley right in at the deep end, having picked the Cheltenham College centre to face Northampton at Franklin's Gardens before he had made an appearance for their second team. Thorley, who had not even played a first-team match for his local club Stow-on-the-Wold, became the youngest player to represent Gloucester in the professional era at 17 years and 56 days. Thorley found himself partnering World Cup-winner Mike Tindall and admitted he was a little star-struck in the 33-6 defeat. 'I didn't think I did too badly but it was just fantastic to play alongside players you had always watched like Mike Tindall and Freddie Burns,' Thorley said.

Thorley may have been nervous but he managed to maintain his composure and won praise from Andrew Stanley, Gloucester's forwards coach. 'You would struggle to guess that Ollie has just turned 17. He mixed in very well with other players and made a couple of nice half breaks and stood up to the physical aspects of the game,' he said.

The award of LV= Breakthrough Player went to another Ollie, Bath's utility back Ollie Devoto, who became the third winner after Gloucester's Jonny May and Exeter's Jack Nowell.

Toulon Too Good
the 2013-14 Heineken Cup

by **DAVID HANDS**

'Wilkinson, 35 the next day, kicked the conversions of tries by Matt Giteau and Juan Smith (in both of which he had a hand), added two penalties and a dropped goal'

It is hard to know where to celebrate the 2013-14 European season first. We can look back at the last of 19 years of the Heineken Cup and treasure what that competition has brought to northern hemisphere rugby. We can look forward to the new three-tier arrangement, headed by the European Rugby Champions Cup, which comes into play in 2014-15.

There was joy for France and England, in that Toulon completed back-to-back wins in the Heineken Cup but that, for the first time since 2011, an English club – Saracens – reached the final and another, London Wasps, ensured seven English clubs would contest the new elite competition.

Or we can take it to a personal level (which is the last thing he would want) and wonder at the end to Jonny Wilkinson's stellar career. Within the space of eight days, Wilkinson raised two trophies as captain of the Toulon team that beat Saracens 23-6 in the Heineken Cup and then carried off the Bouclier de Brennus by defeating Castres in the Top 14 final.

Wilkinson, England's World Cup winner in 2003, suffered such trauma during his career that a triumphal rush at the end of it could be applauded by friend and foe. Yet spare a thought for another 35-year-old who also retired from rugby with nothing to show for one last season of toil: Steve

Borthwick, captain of the Saracens team that lost to Toulon and then lost to Northampton in the Aviva Premiership final.

The wider picture must come first. After months of wrangling in committee rooms, the stakeholders agreed a revised formula for European competition which gives the participating clubs far more responsibility for the commercial success of the tournament. A new body based in Lausanne, European Professional Club Rugby (EPCR), replaces the union-dominated European Rugby Cup Ltd, which was based in Dublin.

Leading club figures believe that revenue can be increased from £44 million to £70 million and, within the next five years, to £100 million, helping to fund a programme which includes a new third tier of competition, a qualifying tournament for eight to 12 teams from Europe's emerging countries.

But the top rung will be occupied by 20 clubs contesting the Champions Cup, instead of the 24 who competed in the 2013-14 Heineken Cup. The next rung, the European Rugby Challenge Cup, will involve 18 teams rather than 20 and the new EPCR board includes one representative respectively of the Aviva Premiership, the Top 14 and the RaboDirect PRO12 so that the interests of all the leading countries are fairly aired.

It is to the credit of two broadcasting companies, Sky Sports and BT Sport, that they have reached a compromise in screening the new competitions which Mark McCafferty,

LEFT Skipper Jonny Wilkinson and the victorious Toulon team after defeating Saracens 23-6 in the 2014 Heineken Cup final at the Millennium Stadium, Cardiff.

ABOVE Kieran Marmion of Connacht, whose 47th-minute try helped his side to a famous 16-14 win away to Toulouse.

FACING PAGE Paea Fa'anunu cannot stop Niki Goneva from scoring in the last minute to set up a dramatic 15-14 victory for Leicester away to Montpellier.

Premier Rugby's chief executive, said would 'deliver a stronger playing format for everyone. We are now entering a new phase of growth in the club game and, alongside the three professional leagues, we're confident that the new competitions will go from strength to strength, as well as incorporate new markets over time.'

The agreement spans an initial eight-year period and the 2014-15 Champions Cup will involve seven English clubs (Saracens, Bath, Northampton, Leicester, Harlequins, Sale Sharks and London Wasps, who beat Stade Français in the two-legged qualifier), six French (Toulon, Clermont Auvergne, Castres, Racing Métro, Montpellier and Toulouse), three Irish (Munster, Leinster and Ulster), two Welsh (Ospreys and Scarlets), Scotland's Glasgow Warriors, and Treviso (Italy).

But what fun we have had from the old tournament, which took rugby supporters to new territories (the old European tournament started, remember, in 1995 on the Black Sea when Toulouse played Farul Constanta from Romania), gave us the phenomenon that is Munster's Red Army, made us all far less insular and gave us moments of heartwarming brilliance to rival anything seen in the international arena.

A personal memory: the first visit to the Brive bear pit in 1996, in the centre of that French town, when Harlequins were the visitors and 15,000 raucous Frenchmen made speech and thought virtually impossible. It was the moment that assured us something special was happening in European rugby and that, after a hesitant first season when no English clubs competed, we should all climb aboard.

The nineteenth edition had its share of thrills and spills too. If you were watching the first fortnight of pool rounds, you would not have put much money on either Toulon or Saracens reaching the final. After two rounds, Saracens had lost their home game with Toulouse (whom the season overall proved to be something of a fading force) at Wembley and Toulon had gone down away to Cardiff Blues.

Scroll forwards to December and Toulon struggled to beat Exeter Chiefs at Sandy Park, their away form continuing to plague them. Mind you, no club had taken the competition by the scruff of the neck at that stage. If there were plaudits for anyone, it was for the Irish – Leinster arrived at Franklin's Gardens and departed with a crushing 40-7 victory over Northampton while Connacht, unheralded Connacht, came away from Toulouse with a 16-14 win which was one of the great results in Heineken Cup history.

Kieran Marmion, Connacht's scrum half who would be capped by Ireland during the summer, wrote his name into provincial history with his side's try and Dan Parks, the veteran Scotland fly half, kicked 11 points. Leinster, the rich relations, were altogether more sumptuous, Luke Fitzgerald scoring three of the six tries which dissected the Saints, five of them converted by Ian Madigan.

So what do Northampton do? They turn up at the Aviva Stadium a week later and leave Leinster reeling with a smash-and-grab 18-9 win. They out-muscled the Irish: George North – playing centre rather than wing – scored one try and Jamie Elliott ran 95 metres for a second as Leinster sought desperately for the score that would sustain their unbeaten pool record.

Leicester were involved in an equally fraught occasion at Montpellier. Needing a win to keep their quarter-final hopes alive, the Tigers played out a scoreless first half and with less than a minute left trailed 14-8. Then came Niki Goneva with the try which, with Ryan Lamb's angled conversion, earned victory by 15-14.

Leicester were in the same pool as Ulster, who headed into the final fortnight of pool rounds with a perfect four out of four. By the time they had finished, Ulster boasted a perfect six out of six: they beat Montpellier 27-16 at Ravenhill and then disposed of Leicester at Welford Road. Or rather, Ruan Pienaar did, the South African scrum half scoring all his side's points in a 22-19 win.

Saracens, meanwhile, crumbled again to Toulouse and, like Leicester, went through to the last eight as one of the two best runners-up. Toulon had been doing enough to get by and, when the dust settled, France and Ireland had three qualifiers each and England two. At this stage, directors of rugby tell themselves and their players that home advantage is all important so, to counteract that, Saracens took themselves off on a three-day break in New York.

Whatever they munched in the Big Apple, it worked. They beat Ulster, at Ravenhill, 17-15, which reflects as much credit on the hosts as the visitors since Ulster played all but the first four minutes with 14 men. Jared Payne, their full back, was dismissed for a dangerous tackle on Alex Goode, who had to be carried off; but though Saracens forced a 17-9 lead with only 11 minutes remaining, they were living on their nerves as Paddy Jackson kicked two late penalties.

The match also proved that Chris Ashton, scorer of two of the three Saracens tries, was back to international form on the wing. Another Irish challenge succumbed when Leinster lost 29-14 to Toulon at the Stade Félix Mayol, despite Wilkinson hobbling off with a strained

FACING PAGE Clermont's Damien Chouly is halted by Saracens Jacques Burger and Schalk Brits during the first semi-final, at Twickenham.

BELOW Look familiar? Jonny Wilkinson slots a dropped goal in the final at Cardiff.

hamstring, second-half tries from Xavier Chiocci and Drew Mitchell securing the verdict.

Munster, though, kept the flag flying with a 47-23 win at Thomond Park over Toulouse. The Irish province registered six tries against a porous Toulouse defence, one of them going to CJ Stander. The South African came on as a replacement in the back row for Munster's captain, Peter O'Mahony, and, on his twenty-fourth birthday, enjoyed a fine game.

With a half-hour played at the Stade Marcel-Michelin, where they had not lost for 74 games, Clermont Auvergne were 16-0 up against Leicester and cruising. Yet Tigers clung on and, had they not lost Thomas Waldrom to the sin-bin in the final quarter, might have ended Clermont's formidable home run. As it was, Morgan Parra kicked five penalties against three by Owen Williams and the French club won 22-16.

Clermont's day of judgment was just round the corner. They drew Saracens in the semi-finals, the match was played at Twickenham and Clermont were crushed 46-6, a humiliation the like of which they have seldom known. Jacques Burger, the Namibian flanker, tackled everything that moved, Ashton scored another two of Saracens' six tries and everything they touched turned to gold.

Toulon reached the final the hard way. Playing at the Stade Vélodrome in Marseille, they beat Munster 24-16, Wilkinson kicking five penalties and a dropped goal. Munster, reduced to 14 when Keith Earls was in a second-half sin-bin, scored the only try through Simon Zebo but could not find that extra edge of class.

Nor could they find a way round Steffon Armitage, the England flanker in exile with Toulon and happy enough to be there. Armitage, once a Saracen, turned out to be the European Player of the Year and, in the final in Cardiff, Saracens simply could not escape his clutches. There was never any sense that the English club could construct victory, not with Wilkinson bearing a charmed existence.

The fly half, 35 the next day, kicked the conversions of tries by Matt Giteau and Juan Smith (in both of which he had a hand), added two penalties and a dropped goal, against two penalties by Owen Farrell. It is hard to imagine a reshaped European future which does not have Wilkinson in it.

Saints Set Up Double
the 2013-14 Amlin Challenge Cup
by TERRY COOPER

'Ben Foden emerged from under a pile of bodies to claim the try. Myler's missed conversion was irrelevant – he had already contributed 20 points'

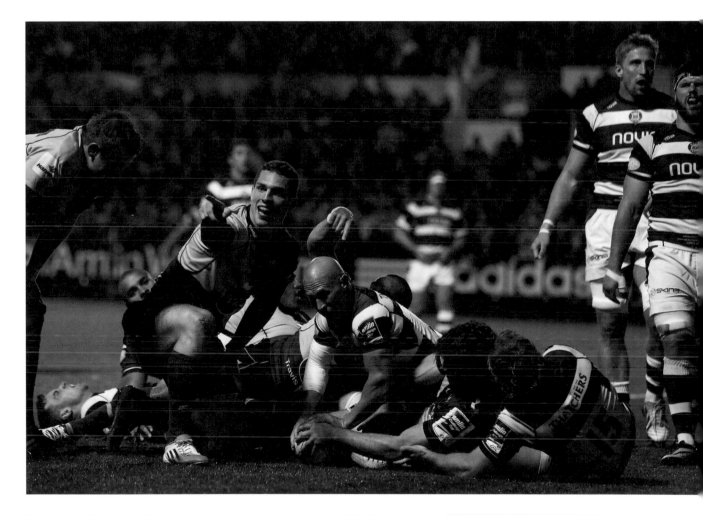

B oth Bath and Northampton entered this Amlin Challenge Cup final with not so much monkeys on their backs but more like giant-sized gorillas. Northampton had competed in four finals in recent seasons and lost the lot, including two LV= Cups (being defeated by Exeter in this season's event), one Heineken Cup and one Premiership. They were in this competition after being a lucky loser when they failed to qualify for the Heineken Cup knockout stage.

ABOVE Full back Ben Foden (second from right on ground) touches down for Northampton's second try of the 2014 Amlin Challenge Cup final.

RIGHT Micky Young spins the ball out in the direction of fly half George Ford as Bath go on the attack at Cardiff Arms Park.

Bath had appeared in 14 semi-finals since winning the Heineken Cup in 1998 and the hope and expectation generated by such progress had resulted in a solitary trophy (the 2007-08 European Challenge Cup). And Bath went in with the recent dejection of not qualifying for the Premiership play-offs, despite being in the top four virtually all season.

Still, at least the match would produce an English winner in a tournament that had become a near monopoly. From 2001 to 2013 an English club had taken the prize nine times – Harlequins three, Sale twice, Wasps, Gloucester and both this season's finalists.

As usual, the unlamented ERC had arranged a final without the slightest regard for the travelling fans of the participants. ERC officials wanted to be on the spot in Cardiff for the big event the day after, so this final was played at the Arms Park, a drop-kick from the Millennium Stadium, where Saints collapsed so traumatically in the 2011 Heineken final against Leinster. So two of the most passionate groups of supporters in England had to travel to another country and, unless they drove, had to stay overnight at exorbitant cost because there are no trains home after a match starting at 8pm.

The opening half contained only one try but was a truly entertaining spectacle. Some of the best attackers in the Premiership were given the opportunity to test the toughest tacklers, who responded by hitting their targets. The tactical kicking, especially by Bath's George Ford, surpassed most of the aimless hoofing that is commonplace in regular league combat. Ford drilled kicks 60 yards downfield, using the skiddy, drenched surface of the artificial pitch to perfection. The pitch was only slightly squishy, despite days of heavy rain in Cardiff, and that stressed that the future is fake grass. Swamps are not for artistic rugby players.

Importantly, referee Jérôme Garcès ran the contest with unflamboyant efficiency, reinforcing the view that French referees have risen from being unpredictable to the best in the world. At least M Garcès did not bark coaching commands to every player who had the temerity to go near the ball.

Ford had made the pragmatic decision to give his damaged shoulder one last hit and have the necessary operation and pull out of the England tour to New Zealand. During his commanding first half he showed what England might lack in All Black-land by thumping in a penalty from 57 yards before two minutes had elapsed.

In the seventh minute Stephen Myler put Northampton in business with a short-range penalty. Ford, the Rugby Players' Association Young Player of the Year, restored Bath's lead in the 13th minute. Northampton levelled six minutes later after two scrums on the Bath line, with the defenders happy to concede just three points.

Bath were still under the hammer in the 27th minute when two special acts swept them back in front. Saints wing Ken Pisi has hardly been tackled harder than the hit by centre Jonathan Joseph, who turned his target into a right-angled rugby player. Pisi, though driven back five yards, still had the dexterity and strength to lay the ball back from the collision. But his colleagues reacted to the availability of the loose ball far slower than Anthony Watson. The Bath wing added to his reputation as a devastating finisher by appearing on the blind side of the tackle site to pilfer the ball and sprint 70 yards with no challengers close. Ford converted and 13-6 was bonus territory for Bath, and it would have been a more cheery interval if Ford had not hooked an inviting penalty in the last minute of the half. That was ominous, because when Ford placed the ball on that kicking tee that was as good as it got for Bath. In fact, it rapidly became very bad, as Ford, the red-hot kicker of the opening half, looked like a novice hit-and-hoper in the second. His failures in front of goal seemed

to affect his general play, as he was involved in a couple of almost comical communication misunderstandings with Nick Abendanon.

But his collapse was not the first hint that Bath were going to be complicit in their own downfall. In the second minute after the interval, Northampton prop Alex Corbisiero, making his first start for six months, was sin-binned for a late challenge on Stuart Hooper. In an extraordinary comment, he said to the referee, 'I'll take the yellow,' as if he had any choice in the matter.

Bath made less than nothing of their one-man advantage, losing the ten-minute spell 3-0. Ford missed with straightforward penalties in the 44th and 48th minutes. In between, Myler landed a long goal. By the hour, Myler had landed an even longer shot from 50 yards and another to put Northampton in front at 15-13 when Ford and Abendanon played with such disharmony that they looked as though they had never been introduced to each other. At the start of the last quarter Myler's supreme accuracy extended Northampton's lead to 18-13, though Ford mastered his fragile nerves to land an easy kick – as if there were such a thing in his transformed state of mind.

At 16-18 Bath were still in the hunt, but they proceeded to give Saints another nudge when substitute prop Anthony Perenise was sent to the bin for a ruck offence in the 70th minute. Instantly Northampton cashed in on their superior numbers with a maul-over try dotted down by Phil Dowson. Myler converted and added to his influence on Northampton's magnificent second half by intercepting a pass given by, inevitably, the now inept Ford on his own 22. Myler's steal from his rival stand-off was symbolic of the shift in their fortunes from first half to second. Myler doesn't have the gas to stay clear of the pursuit for 75 yards, but he found support. He handed on to Ken Pisi, who fed Luther Burrell, but he stumbled with the line beckoning. But Ben Foden emerged from under a pile of bodies to claim the try. Myler's missed conversion was irrelevant – he had already contributed 20 points.

Northampton rugby director Jim Mallinder is President of the Myler Appreciation Society and he said, 'You need a performance like that in big games – just somebody who can keep his head and make really good decisions, not just kicking his goals. But he did that as well. It was top drawer by Stephen on a night when all our leaders stepped up.

'We had a game plan that involved moving their front five around. As a team we're improving. We're better than last year and are pleased with the way we are going.'

Myler commented, 'You have to earn trophies, and our forwards have been outstanding all season for us. They have given us a platform to play from. But we did have to regroup at half-time.'

Captain Tom Wood added, 'It wasn't alarm bells at half-time, but it's always frustrating to be behind. But we were confident that we had it in the tank to finish the job.'

Bath head coach Mike Ford, father of George, acknowledged, 'We had to take our opportunities when they were on offer, but we missed a couple, while Myler picked us off. Maybe at crucial times the inner belief that you get from winning big games and trophies just wasn't quite there because we have no history of that.

'We're proud of what we have done this season. We're not going to change our philosophy, because we have got one of the best packs in the country, if not the best, and a massively exciting back line. We don't want anyone to feel sorry for us.'

Bath captain Stuart Hooper stated, 'We played perfect cup final rugby in the first half. The way you are judged in sport is by winning trophies. In the cold light of day we will look back at the improvements we have made this season and the way the young guys are getting better.'

No one knows *income* territory like our PROFIT hunters.

THE ARTEMIS income hunters are experts in their field. Indeed they know income territory like the proverbial back of their hand. Long famed for their Equity Income Profits, in recent years our hunters have also been bagging Bond Income Profits. Even bringing home mixed bags of Equity Income and Bond Income Profits. And now they hunt across the world map, training their sights on the coveted Global Income Profit too. Please remember that past performance should not be seen as a guide to future performance. The value of an investment and any income from it can fall as well as rise as a result of market and currency fluctuations and you may not get back the amount originally invested.

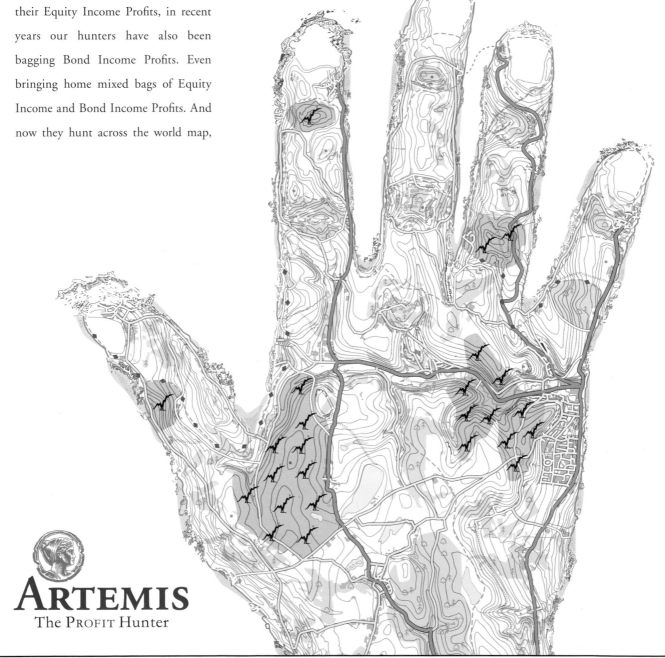

ARTEMIS
The PROFIT Hunter

0800 092 2051   *investorsupport@artemisfunds.com*   *artemis.co.uk*

Issued by Artemis Fund Managers Limited which is authorised and regulated by the Financial Conduct Authority (www.fca.org.uk), 25 The North Colonnade, Canary Wharf, London E14 5HS. For your protection calls are usually recorded. Contains Ordnance Survey data © Crown copyright and database right 2014.

REVIEW OF THE
SEASON 2013-14

Bod's Last Hurrah
the 2014 Six Nations
Championship
by CHRIS JONES

'Damien Chouly was convinced he had won it for France late on, but the final pass was ruled forward. The title was Ireland's to provide O'Driscoll with a wonderful send-off'

The scene was understandably subdued. Standing around in their dinner suits were the England players who had earlier defeated Italy 52-11 to give themselves the chance to lift the Six Nations title for the first time since 2011. However, they had to wait until the end of Ireland's match in France to discover if their Triple Crown triumph was to be followed by the tournament title. Ireland knew exactly what they had to do to win the championship and no matter how you look at it, that gave the Irish an advantage. It appeared that the England players milling around an ancient hall near the Vatican – where their post-match dinner was taking place – would

be receiving one of the Six Nations trophies that are made available when multiple winning scenarios are played out, but it was quickly packed away and the live television links cancelled when Ireland registered a 22-20 victory in Paris to win the title.

Members of the England squad had been cheering as France appeared to have won the game to give the Rose Rose men the triumph, but the try was called back and Ireland were able to give Brian O'Driscoll the perfect end to a stellar career. His retirement party went on long into the night as the Irish enjoyed a moment that England knew could have been their own Grand Slam triumph. The previous season Wales had destroyed England's Slam hopes in emphatic style; however, this time it was by their own deeds that the English failed to win the ultimate northern hemisphere accolade.

Two capricious bounces of the ball in the first quarter of their opening Six Nations match with France resulted in home tries, and with replacement Gaël Fickou scoring the late winner, it was the French who triumphed 26-24 on the first day of what turned out to be a marvellous tournament. As the party fell desperately flat in Rome, England head coach Stuart Lancaster talked about the improvements his team had made, the new players who had emerged like Luther Burrell and the consistently brilliant form shown by full back Mike Brown, who would be named RBS Six Nations Player of the Championship, having been similarly lauded after his QBE Autumn International performances.

Despite another second-place finish, wins over Ireland, Scotland, Wales and Italy confirmed England's position as serious challengers for the 2015 Rugby World Cup they will host, although this

ABOVE Replacement Gaël Fickou is about to touch down to bring the scores level at 24-24 and set up victory for France against England in Paris.

FACING PAGE All over: Brian O'Driscoll celebrates victory and the Six Nations title at the Stade de France at the end of his 141st and final Test match.

optimism took a jolt in the summer when the All Blacks won the three-match series against captain Chris Robshaw and his men 3-0.

While Ireland, France and England had ensured it was a nail-biting end to the championship, the other teams had been playing for pride and it turned out to be a campaign of mixed success for Wales, who had been hoping to make history with a third successive triumph. They were hampered by injuries and mounting concern that some of their senior forwards were getting close to their sell-by date. France were, yet again, ridiculously inconsistent, failing to build on that early triumph over England and seem no nearer a settled side under Philippe Saint-André, their tinkering coach, even though they were in the title mix at the death.

Scotland played out their final season with Scott Johnson as coach, but he has now moved upstairs, allowing Vern Cotter to take over after an impressive period with Clermont Auvergne, and their summer Test wins in North and South America were encouraging. Italy finished winless and like Wales have the problem of filling the gaps left by ageing forwards. They have back-line talent, including Tommy Allan, but have little strength in depth, which is worrying.

On the opening Six Nations weekend, tries from Alex Cuthbert and Scott Williams saw Wales register a 23-15 win over Italy at the Millennium Stadium, and Leigh Halfpenny was impressive with the

LEFT Eye on the ball. George North challenges Angelo Esposito (left) and Josh Furno as Wales defeat Italy at the Millennium Stadium.

FACING PAGE Full back Mike Brown, Player of the Championship, passes his Scotland opposite number Stuart Hogg to score in England's 20-0 win at Murraryfield.

boot once again – and they needed his skill as the visitors came back to 20-15 at one stage to highlight weaknesses in the home team's game.

In Paris the home side had led 16-3 after just 22 minutes thanks to two tries from Yoann Huget, but England responded with tries from Mike Brown and Luther Burrell, making his debut. A Danny Care dropped goal and a penalty from replacement Alex Goode had given England a 24-19 advantage, only for Fickou to cut through; Maxime Machenaud's conversion sealed a dramatic win for Les Bleus.

Irish fans in Dublin were making the most of O'Driscoll's final games and were delighted to see Scotland beaten 28-6 at the Aviva Stadium with tries from Andrew Trimble, Jamie Heaslip and Rob Kearney. Heaslip led the side after Paul O'Connell was injured before match day and it was an encouraging start for new coach Joe Schmidt, while O'Driscoll won a record-breaking 129th cap for Ireland.

England defeated a limited Scotland team without any trouble 20-0 at Murrayfield to highlight the paucity of Scottish attacking weapons; no one could understand why they had dropped captain Kelly Brown, which proved to be a major error of judgment by Johnson. Scotland were kept scoreless against England for the first time since 1978. Building on their earlier win over England, France made easy work of Italy, winning 30-10, with Louis Picamoles, Wesley Fofana and Hugo Bonneval scoring early in the second half to settle the match as a contest, although Tommaso Iannone scored for the visitors.

Having gone down 26-3 in Dublin in the second round of matches, Wales, with tries from George North and Sam Warburton along with 17 points from the boot of Leigh Halfpenny, kept their hopes of retaining their RBS 6 Nations title alive with a 27-6 win over France on a Friday night in Cardiff. Duncan Weir's last-gasp dropped goal earned a 21-20 victory over Italy for Scotland, who clinched a first win in Rome since 2006 and ensured they had a really great chance of avoiding the Wooden Spoon. Hardly a reason to celebrate too hard! Josh Furno's late try, converted by Luciano Orquera, had appeared to give Italy the victory, but then Weir had the last word for the Scots.

The standard of play was much higher at Twickenham where a Danny Care breakaway try saw England emerge 13-10 winners over Ireland. The Irish had led 10-3 through Rob Kearney's try, but then England saw Care race in under the posts and Owen Farrell convert, and Irish Triple Crown and Grand Slam hopes were over for O'Driscoll. That disappointment was soon erased for Irish fans as he marked his final game in Dublin by helping Ireland hammer Italy 46-7, setting a new world cap record with his 140th international appearance (including eight for the Lions).

Scottish hopes that their Italy win would herald a new dawn proved painfully false as a Jean-Marc Doussain late penalty saw France snatch a 19-17 victory at Murrayfield. It meant the French would also be in the title hunt in Paris, although the Irish and English were the shorter-odds winners of this three-way shoot-out at the end of a great championship campaign. England ensured they would be full of confidence going to Rome by clinching the Triple Crown by exacting revenge

on Wales for their loss 12 months earlier when hunting the Slam in Cardiff. Tries from Danny Care and Luther Burrell allied to Owen Farrell's kicking – he gathered 19 points – earned a 29-18 victory.

And so it came down to the final Saturday, and while all the games were on the same day, television schedules called for three successive matches, with England the early kick-off in Rome. Mike Brown crossed twice, while further tries from Owen Farrell, Jack Nowell, Mako Vunipola, Manu Tuilagi and Chris Robshaw meant a thumping 52-11 win. George North and Jamie Roberts scored two tries each as Wales recorded a record-breaking 51-3 victory against 14-man Scotland, who had full back Stuart Hogg red-carded for his late shoulder charge on Dan Biggar after 23 minutes.

That just left the France v Ireland match in Paris, the visitors holding on for their 22-20 title-winning victory. Jonathan Sexton scored two tries, while Andrew Trimble grabbed one. However, France followed Brice Dulin's first-half try with a Dimitri Szarzewski score, and then Damien Chouly was convinced he had won it for France late on, but the final pass was ruled forward. England's party was ruined and the title was Ireland's to provide O'Driscoll with a wonderful send-off.

ABOVE Back-row Damien Chouly thinks he has snatched the final game for France, but a forward pass invalidated the try, and the title was Ireland's.

FACING PAGE Smiles all round as Duncan Weir wins the game for Scotland against Italy in Rome with a 40-metre dropped goal as full-time beckoned.

The Club Scene
England: Oh, Bristol!

by NEALE HARVEY

'Controversy aside, the Championship continues to go from strength to strength and one wonders how long it will be before full professionalism is achieved'

It was meant to be their year. Everything was in place: a big-name new director of rugby in former England and Scotland boss Andy Robinson, assisted by former Ospreys boss Sean Holley; superb backing from benefactor-in-chief Steve Lansdown; a squad to die for; and a move across the city to Ashton Gate in the offing after 93 years at the historic Memorial Ground. Surely the Greene King IPA Championship title and a long-awaited place in the Premiership would be theirs?

Alas, it was not to be. Having finished top of the pile by a clear eight points then battled past Rotherham in the play-off semi-finals to set up a home-and-away denouement with London Welsh, Robinson's men fluffed their lines. After a 27-8 defeat in a rain-affected first leg at the Kassam Stadium, Oxford, Bristol briefly threatened a revival in the sold-out return, but eventually subsided to a 20-21 defeat and must now face a sixth successive season outside the top flight.

RIGHT Rotherham's Juan Pablo Socino in action against Bristol in the Championship semi-finals. Socino, the division's Player of the Season, has moved to Newcastle Falcons for 2014-15.

FACING PAGE Seb Stegmann is mobbed after scoring for London Welsh in the second leg of the Championship final against Bristol.

It is the third time Bristol have topped the Championship table and failed in the play-offs, which brings into question the validity of a system that punishes success. As Lansdown, who made his pile in financial services before donating a fair chunk of his personal wealth to save Bristol in 2011, said in the depressing aftermath: 'You can't describe the feeling in a situation like this because you play all season to win a league, then go into a play-off situation and get knocked out.

'I know it's over two legs but it's a one-off situation and that can't be right when you're investing into a club in the way I have to get yourself to the higher levels. Rugby needs to have a close look at this really because it's simply wrong. If two went up and, as in football, you had a play-off for the second spot, fair enough, the team that wins the league would go up. But where we are now means we've got to come back and do it again next year, which is difficult to accept.'

Lansdown has a point and the authorities should take note. Can the game afford to diminish the enthusiasm of a man who is prepared to invest the way he has? Of course not.

Controversy aside, the Championship continues to go from strength to strength and one wonders how long it will be before full professionalism is achieved. Rotherham were the surprise packages, achieving a top-four spot under their ambitious new young head coach Lee Blackett by playing an energetic brand of attacking rugby that attracted many plaudits, while the heartening revival story that is London Scottish continued with a highly creditable fifth-place finish.

Bedford, habitual play-off contenders over the previous four years, were surprisingly off colour and flirted with relegation before finishing ninth, while Nottingham fell off their perch to end up tenth. The dreaded demotion spot eventually boiled down to a battle between Ealing, who were competing in the second tier for the first time after a remarkable ascent from the London Leagues, and Jersey, who needed to win at Bedford on the final day whilst hoping Ealing lost at home to Rotherham. And it was the Channel Islanders who eventually prevailed, with their 41-31 win combined with a 29-36 loss for Ealing securing another year of tier-two rugby.

The race for the National League One title was no less dramatic, with season-long favourites Doncaster digging a huge hole for themselves by losing at challengers Rosslyn Park four rounds

from the end of the season. Doncaster having invested heavily in maintaining a full-time squad following the previous year's demotion from the Championship, failure to win promotion to the second tier at the first attempt might have proved disastrous. There was no room for error ahead of Donny's last three matches, but victories over Wharfedale and Coventry set up a last-day decider at Blackheath and Clive Griffiths' men clinched the title with a bruising 38-20 victory.

Down at the wrong end, it was notable that all three sides promoted from National League Two the previous season – Henley Hawks, Worthing and Hull Ionians – immediately went back down, which highlights the increasing strength of National League One.

If drama is your thing, the promotion race from National Two North surpassed anything you are likely to see at any level of the game, anywhere in the world. Heading into the final Saturday of the regular season, three sides were still in contention for the title, with leaders Macclesfield needing a minimum of two points from their trip to nearest rivals Darlington Mowden Park who, like third-placed Stourbridge, started the day four points in arrears of the Blues.

ABOVE Lancashire No. 8 Matthew Lamprey scores one of his county's four second-half tries against Cornwall at Twickenham.

RIGHT Kent with the County Championship Division 2 Plate after beating Durham 31-23 in the final.

A bumper crowd of 3750 spectators turned out at Darlington's Northern Echo Arena for their title decider with Macclesfield and were treated to an epic battle that went right down to the wire. Darlington established a 28-12 lead after an hour, but Macclesfield pulled one back and then claimed both the try and losing bonus points they needed in stoppage time.

Macclesfield were crowned champions, while Darlington settled for a play-off for the second promotion spot against Ampthill. And they looked set for further heartbreak when Ampthill led with just seconds remaining, before scrum half Zylon McGaffin squeezed through the narrowest of gaps to score the winning try and send Darlo up with the last throw of the dice.

Hartpury College, who enjoy close ties with Premiership side Gloucester and share the same facilities, continued their rise by clinching the National Two South title with eight points to spare over Ampthill. Hartpury's ascension means there are now two full-blown student sides in National League One, where long-time rivals Loughborough lie in wait. Ampthill may have failed in their quest for promotion, but there was joy for one of their top performers, full back Elliot Clements-Hill, whose 20 tries and 350 points earned him a move to Championship side Plymouth.

Lydney, who are coached these days by former Bath and England prop Duncan Bell, are heading back to level four after wrapping up National Three South West by an impressive 19 points, while the other divisional winners at level five were Dorking (London & South East), Huddersfield (North) and Broadstreet (Midlands). Joining them in National Two are play-off winners Stockport and Old Elthamians, who defeated Redingensians and Sutton Coldfield respectively.

Trowbridge, coached by former Bath and England flanker Steve Ojomoh, lifted the RFU Intermediate Cup by defeating Leek 22-19 in a nail-biting encounter at Twickenham, while there was a Gloucestershire double in both the RFU Senior and Junior Vases, with Newent's 'Green Army' defeating Yarnbury 20-13 to claim the former and Longlevens beating a revitalised Rugby Lions 23-12 to lift the latter – fine achievements for those famous West Country clubs.

The County Championship continues its welcome rise in popularity and, in a repeat of last year's final, Lancashire defended their title with a 36-26 victory over a well-supported Cornwall. Surrey completed a Shield final hat-trick by defeating Leicestershire 39-16, while Kent ran in four tries to beat Durham 31-23 to lift the Plate. It capped a fine season all round.

Scotland: Glasgow So Close

by ALAN LORIMER

'Russell was probably the find of the season at Glasgow, the former Stirling County youth player emerging from the shadow of Scotland caps Duncan Weir and Ruaridh Jackson'

If Scottish rugby needed a lift after a depressing Six Nations season, then Glasgow Warriors provided the required tonic by reaching the final of the RaboDirect PRO12 even if it all ended in defeat to Leinster at the RDS in Dublin.

This was the first time Glasgow Warriors had reached the final of the play-offs, but it came as no surprise to a growing army of fans, who had applauded head coach Gregor Townsend's bold style of

play, his careful of rotation of players, his blooding of a number of youngsters – and most of all, nine straight wins leading up to the final.

Townsend's side finished second in the league table to Leinster but boasted the highest number of wins. That second place gave Glasgow a home semi-final in the play-offs against Munster and in the event it proved crucial as the Warriors held off a late challenge by their Irish opponents to win 16-15. But in the final against Leinster in Dublin two weeks later, Warriors made too many mistakes against their seasoned rivals and despite being in contention at half-time eventually suffered a 34-12 defeat.

Warriors' performance, however, stirred the soul of Scottish rugby to the extent that even the more staid folk of Edinburgh could be heard belting out the words of the 1920 Will Fyffe song 'I Belong to Glasgow', now the signature anthem at Warriors' Scotstoun stadium.

Glasgow's campaign was about more than reaching the final of the play-offs. As a Scottish Rugby Union-owned club Glasgow are committed to providing and developing players for the national team. And there is little doubt that Townsend succeeded in this objective, with a number of players forcing their way into Scotland's summer tour squad.

Among these are prop Gordon Reid, lock Jonny Gray, stand-off Finn Russell and centre Mark Bennett. Russell was probably the find of the season at Glasgow, the former Stirling County youth

player emerging from the shadow of Scotland caps Duncan Weir and Ruaridh Jackson to become the first choice in the 10 position.

Nor did Townsend stop there. His insistence that current form was what mattered meant that Peter Murchie was chosen for the semi final and final ahead of Stuart Hogg in the full-back position. Townsend also showed smart judgment in the foreign players he brought into the Glasgow squad, notably the effervescent Niko Matawalu, albeit the Fijian, a cult figure at Scotstoun, was culpable of costly errors in the Dublin final.

Glasgow's best ball carrier was South African Josh Strauss, who after three years with the Warriors is now eligible to play for Scotland. And Scotland might as well take the opportunity of playing the South African, if only to follow the lead of just about every other country in filling up with foreigners!

If there was a feeling of success at Glasgow, then over in the East of Scotland a decidedly different atmosphere prevailed. Edinburgh had ditched Irishman Michael Bradley as head coach and then appointed Alan Solomons. The South African, however, was not able to be in place for the pre-season nor indeed for the first few league matches, and inevitably teething problems ensued.

Soon after arriving at Murrayfield, Solomons hired a number of his fellow countrymen and with overseas signings bequeathed to him from

LEFT Glasgow Warriors fly half Finn Russell shoots for goal in the RaboDirect PRO12 semi-final v Munster at Scotstoun. Russell kicked 11 of Warriors' 16 points as they progressed to the final.

the Bradley era Edinburgh began to have a distinctly non-Scottish appearance. Whether that affected the esprit is arguable, but the results suggest some malaise present in the squad.

Admittedly Solomons was unlucky with season-long injuries to the likes of star winger Tim Visser. Moreover the head coach, insistent that Greig Laidlaw remained at scrum half, found that he lacked a top-class stand-off. In a shrewd rejigging, Solomons switched Greig Tonks from full back to the 10 position, the move bringing immediate success. Sadly the experiment ended when Tonks was injured playing for Scotland A against England A and remained out of action for the rest of the season.

If, as it seems, Solomons had missed the boat on signings for last year, he avoided any tardiness this season by securing the services of Tom Heathcote from Bath to replace the outgoing stand-offs Harry Leonard and Gregor Hunter. Additionally Solomons has invested in home talent by signing the Gala props Ewan McQuillin and Rory Sutherland and the Melrose winger Damien Hoyland.

Edinburgh, despite a dismal season in the RaboDirect PRO12 league, did at least achieve several results in the Heineken Cup, with wins over Munster, Gloucester and Perpignan, but that was little consolation for a lowly eighth finish in their bread-and-butter competition.

In contrast to Glasgow's compact stadium at Scotstoun, Edinburgh have been forced to play their matches in the 67,500-seat mausoleum that is Murrayfield. That changed, however, when the SRU ploughed up the infested Murrayfield grass ahead of installing a new hybrid pitch, resulting in Edinburgh decamping to the more intimate surroundings of Meggetland, the home of Boroughmuir.

The 3000-capacity ground seemed to be the answer to Edinburgh's needs and the club duly celebrated the move with a 31-25 win over Ospreys. But that proved merely a blip. A few weeks later Munster knocked on the head any notion of an Edinburgh revival with a 55-12 trouncing of the Scottish capital side to expose Edinburgh's problems in giant writing.

Edinburgh's weakness last season, and indeed the problems of the national side, again brought calls for a third professional team to be reinstated in Scotland. It seemed the financial muscle of oil-rich Aberdeen might provide the wherewithal to fund a third side, but this proved to be a non-starter and for the moment it looks as though Scotland will continue to struggle with a base of professional players too small to adequately underpin an international team.

Many would argue that there are simply not enough quality players in the system to justify a third team. But there is ample evidence to suggest that within the Premiership, the top layer of amateur rugby in Scotland, there are players good enough to become professionals. Edinburgh's most successful backs, Matt Scott and Doug Fife, both graduated from the Currie club, and looking further back Kelly Brown played for Melrose before securing a contract with the Borders district side.

There is much talk of trying to bridge the gap between the professional game and the Premiership. That involves semi-professionalism, but as yet the idea is too vague to be implemented and moreover has yet to be accepted by many of the amateur clubs.

Scotland's Premiership clubs do provide a good proving ground for young players, but to suggest that they are anywhere near professional standard would be wide of the mark. Just look at what happened in the British & Irish Cup last season when Gala lost 86-8 to Leeds in the opening round, a mismatch that has prompted calls for Scotland to be represented by Glasgow A and Edinburgh A in the competition.

Significantly Melrose, who finished outside the top four in 2012-13 and hence did not qualify for the British & Irish Cup, were much stronger last season in domestic competition as a result of not having to punch above their weight playing against bigger and heavier professional sides in the cross-border competition.

That kept Melrose fresher than their rivals and it was no surprise that the Premiership title returned to the Greenyards. Melrose, under new coach John Dalziel, played a brand of rugby that was both attractive and effective and at the end of a long season they were once again champions, edging out their near Border neighbours, Gala.

At the other end of the table travel-weary Aberdeen were relegated, swapping places with Boroughmuir, but Edinburgh Accies, who were second from bottom, costing the coaching team their positions, survived the drop after winning the play-off against Stewart's Melville.

Meanwhile in the cup Glasgow Hawks showed their resurgence by reaching the final with an injury-time penalty goal from the halfway line against Gala in the penultimate round. But in the final, played at Cumbernauld on plastic, it was a display of fast and ultimately winning rugby by Heriot's that brought the cup back to Goldenacre.

Wales: Plus Ça Change

by DAVID STEWART

'With only the top six teams in the Rabo qualifying for the new senior European competition, Welsh representation is reduced to two, their lowest so far'

A year ago we reported upon a weak performance by the regional teams, strife between them and the union leading to a former WRU chief popping up from New Zealand to lobby on behalf of the regions, and key players leaving to play their club rugby elsewhere. *Plus ça change, plus c'est la même chose.*

Once again no Welsh team made it to the quarter-finals of the Heineken, but this time – worse – neither did any feature in the play-off stage of the RaboDirect PRO12 or the semi-finals of the LV= Cup. The financial dispute rolled on, and David Moffett resurfaced in his 'mischief making' campaign (the description of present CEO Roger Lewis) against his former employers, culminating in an EGM where the WRU had to face down a 'no-confidence' motion. For good measure Leigh

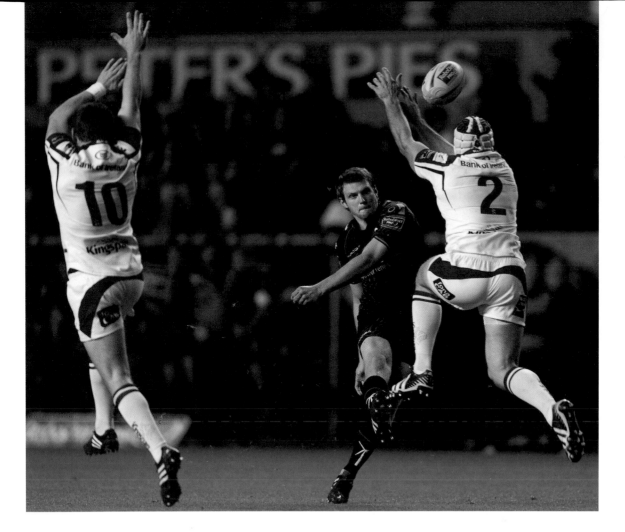

Halfpenny and Jonathan Davies joined the exodus to France, meaning that with Richard Hibbard heading for Gloucester, more than half the current national side are playing outside Wales. Happy days, not.

The Ospreys secured the highest league position, fifth, missing a play-off spot by four points. The Scarlets were 11 points behind in sixth. With only the top six teams in the Rabo qualifying for the new senior European competition, Welsh representation is reduced to two, their lowest so far. As Irish provinces occupy three of the top four slots, it is instructive to examine those head-to-head contests. The Ospreys managed only one win from six contests against Leinster, Munster and Ulster (one from eight if we include Glasgow Warriors, runners-up in the league), whereas they recorded five from six against the other Welsh regions, with only the Blues avoiding a clean sweep. A sting in the tail of their season was a 30-27 defeat at Zebre in their penultimate game.

Most disappointing of all was coming bottom of their – admittedly tough – pool in the Heineken Cup. Their campaign was derailed in the first round by losing 19-9 to Leinster at the Liberty Stadium. They finished with a solitary home win against Castres (21-12) in the credit column.

Only a few seasons ago their team sheet was virtually a full international XV, but with Hibbard, Ryan Jones and Ian Evans heading east of Offa's Dyke, the pack now has a much less experienced look. Their best move was re-signing the excellent Alun Wyn Jones whose display of loyalty to city and country is to be admired. Dan Biggar attracted recognition from elsewhere in being voted the RaboDirect PRO12 Players' Player of the Year. Canadian wing Jeff Hassler was a welcome addition, and Dan Baker made sufficient progress to become back-up No. 8 on the national side by the end-of-season tour to South Africa.

ABOVE Ospreys' Dan Biggar, Players' Player of the Year in the PRO12, has a dropped goal charged down against Ulster at the Liberty Stadium.

FACING PAGE Replacement fly half Gareth Davies touches down the deciding try as Cardiff Blues beat eventual tournament winners Toulon 19-15 in the Heineken Cup pool stages.

The Scarlets' season was founded on a renewed forward effort, having discovered the new scrum engagement to their liking and developed an effective rolling maul. Key in this were new Welsh caps Rhodri Jones and Samson Lee at prop and Jake Ball in the second row. Exciting influences behind include scrum halves Gareth Davies and Rhodri Williams, and Jordan Williams on the left flank, whose elegant evasive running evokes much of Shane Williams; all three won first caps.

Home wins against Ulster (17-9) and Munster (18-13) were the only successes against the Irish/Glasgow top four, accounting for their mid-table finish. Their Heineken Cup started brightly enough with a performance of high skill and pace at Harlequins (won 33-26), followed by a home draw against Racing Métro (26-26). They also managed to overcome Racing away (19-13) but finished in third place in Pool Four.

With the loss of Jonathan Davies, and the pursuit of Simon Easterby and Danny Wilson by Ireland and Bristol, those in the west will fear they have become a 'selling club' in soccer parlance. Auckland's experienced Wayne Pivac bolsters the coaching roster in a rare but perhaps inevitable departure from the 'promote from within' philosophy. Exciting wing Harry Robinson is an interesting capture from Cardiff Blues.

The Blues had a season to forget. A run of poor form and weak results saw director of rugby Phil Davies part company with the club in March. His assistants from Pontypridd, Paul John and Dale McIntosh, looked after playing affairs to the end of the season, and will continue under Mark Hammett from Wellington Hurricanes. An early indication of the struggles to come was a first home defeat to Zebre (30-25) in September (for good measure, they lost the return in March, 15-10). The most remarkable week came in the Heineken: their first pool game saw a hammering by Exeter Chiefs 44-29 (a strong second-half rally avoiding a much poorer scoreline), yet the following weekend they beat the eventual champions Toulon 19-15.

On the personnel front, talented centre Cory Allen who has the priceless ability to perform in the 12 and 13 jerseys was another to make Wales's summer tour to South Africa, and is a clear challenger for a berth on the national side. Tragically, his highly promising co-centre Owen

Williams suffered a severe spinal injury playing in Singapore after the season's end. Robin Copeland's move to Munster after an outstanding season at No. 8 is a loss.

Dragons started promisingly with wins over Ulster (15-8) and Scarlets (23-16) at Rodney Parade, but come the softer grounds and the impact of injury, their young and small squad began to struggle once more. Particularly disturbing late-season defeats were 24-8 at home to Connacht and 45-27 in Treviso. The installation of canny Lyn Jones as director of rugby, now supported by Kingsley Jones as head coach and Huw Bevan (most recently fitness coach with the England cricket team) and with former Lion Gareth Davies as CEO gives the eastern region some serious operators running the show. Playing additions include former internationals Lee Byrne, Aled Brew, Andy Powell and Ian Gough who should add a layer of much-needed experience.

It is fitting to note the achievement of London Welsh in bouncing back to the English Premiership at the first time of asking, under former Cardiff coach Justin Burnell. More imagination is needed to develop that relationship into something of wider benefit to the game in Wales.

Which brings us back to the politics. The union won a crushing victory in the no-confidence debate which centred round restructuring leagues in the community game. As former Llanelli CEO Stuart Gallacher noted upon his recent retirement from the game, there is clearly a 'positive and progressive agreement' to be grasped, if only both sides can demonstrate the required degree of flexibility and goodwill. That much is owed to all stakeholders within the Welsh game.

It was all too much for the universally admired Gerald Davies who announced he would not seek re-election to the WRU committee, after a final speech where he told some home truths about how his union is viewed around the world – 'not held in high regard'. The reaction of his old colleague Gareth Edwards spoke for so many: 'People wonder why half the time we are always squabbling; why aren't we getting on with the fundamental parts of what the sport is all about'.

Amen to that. One positive sign is a new sponsorship deal between BT and the regions. Maybe the darkest hour is the one just before dawn. Supporters throughout Wales will be hoping so.

next
ARE HAPPY TO SUPPORT

THE WOODEN SPOON
RUGBY WORLD 15

Ireland: An Era Ends

by RUAIDHRI O'CONNOR

'Despite losing Brian O'Driscoll to a calf injury in the final act of his brilliant career just minutes into the game, Leinster turned on the style after half-time'

einster's European dominance may have been broken by Toulon, but in the RaboDirect PRO12 the Irish province continue to rule the roost in relative comfort. It was Matt O'Connor's first season in charge of the three-time Heineken Cup champions, and while the Australian came in for some criticism over his side's style of play during the campaign, there was no doubting their ability to win games and eke out results despite acting as bulk suppliers to the Irish national team throughout the season.

The province's position of pre-eminence in Irish rugby was re-emphasised at the levels below as well, with the 'A' side winning the British & Irish Cup for the second successive season, while the

ABOVE Leinster legends Brian O'Driscoll and Leo Cullen lift the RaboDirect PRO12 trophy after the province's 34-12 win over Glasgow Warriors in the final.

Ulster Bank League title remained in Dublin, with Clontarf becoming, in dramatic circumstances, the fourth different capital city club to claim the All Ireland title.

Not that Leinster's dominance went unchallenged. The balance of power in the PRO12 is currently firmly resting in Ireland, with Munster and Ulster joining their rivals in the play-offs along with Glasgow Warriors. There are question marks over the competition's strength at the current time as the flight of players from Wales to England and France continues to drain the regions, but the fact that the same three provinces reached the European knockout stages underlines their credentials.

Connacht, meanwhile, showed glimpses of promise under new head coach Pat Lam, but those glimpses came all too infrequently and they finished off-the-pace and outside Europe's elite as the restructuring of the continent's competitions added new incentives for the lower-ranked sides.

Munster, in what would prove to be their final season under New Zealander Rob Penney, will reflect on a disappointing campaign. They used an October victory over Glasgow in Scotstoun as a springboard for a long unbeaten run that saw them lead the league for months, but their form deserted them in the run-in, resulting in the Reds being overhauled by the Scots, and that led to their downfall in the semi-finals. There will be much work to do for new coach Anthony Foley.

Ulster's quest for silverware must go on, meanwhile, as they failed to achieve the consistency they managed when topping the table in 2012-13 when redevelopment work on their Ravenhill home meant they ceded advantage to Leinster in the final and lost the game narrowly.

Their neighbours were again their undoing in the play-offs, with Ian Madigan's second-half try helping his side come from 9-0 down to defeat Ulster 13-9 and end Johann Muller, John Afoa and Tom Court's time at the northern province trophyless. They would subsequently be joined at the exit door by director of rugby David Humphreys and coach Mark Anscombe, whose departures both came as shocks after the season had ended.

That uninspiring win set up a final between Leinster and Glasgow, who had overcome Munster the previous evening, with Penney exiting the province fuming over the lack of cameras at Scotstoun where Simon Zebo was denied a try by the television match official who couldn't find a definitive angle. While that had proved crucial, the problems that have plagued the Cantabrian's two seasons in charge of the province were evident in Glasgow as the Warriors marched on backed by a vociferous home crowd.

They brought a big away contingent to Dublin for the RDS final, but despite regularly going toe to toe with Leinster during their regular season match-ups and even the previous year's semi-final, the Irish province were far too strong. Despite losing Brian O'Driscoll to a calf injury in the final act of his brilliant career just minutes into the game, the hosts turned on the style after half-time, with Springbok Zane Kirchner and Ireland hooker Sean Cronin sparkling in a 34-12 win.

Sitting in the stands were three of the men who had played a key role in the campaign to get them there: Dave Kearney was out injured after an outstanding campaign that saw him become an Irish regular, while Noel Reid and Jordi Murphy had contributed hugely during the international windows when O'Connor was reliant on his squad to get points while vast swathes of his playing strength were wearing green.

Lifting the trophy would prove a fitting exit for two club legends, with long-term captain Leo Cullen and Irish great O'Driscoll hanging up their boots after the final, while coaches Greg Feek and Jono Gibbes are moving on to the national set-up and Clermont respectively. They follow last year's departees Joe Schmidt, Johnny Sexton and Isa Nacewa out the door, but the word 'transition' won't be contemplated by those involved at the RDS, where they will seek to continue their drive for success this season.

'That's what the environment expects,' O'Connor said. 'That's what everyone involved has come to expect from Leinster Rugby and from that end nobody has shied away from the expectation and that drives the environment every day to deliver that.

'You can't make it in our environment if you're not a leader. That's the reality, so there are a load of them. You have just got to develop them and grow them and give them the opportunity to be that little bit better.'

He could draw great satisfaction from the province's B&I Cup win, with out-half Cathal Marsh inspiring the second string to a 44-17 win over Leeds Carnegie in the final, with captain Dominic Ryan's side overcoming Munster en route to their success.

Many of the players involved plied their trade in the Ulster Bank League throughout the season, where Clontarf ended their long wait for a title on the final day as they overhauled city rivals Old Belvedere. The northsiders had it all to do going into the last Saturday, with Belvo simply needing to beat relegated Garryowen in Limerick to win the league for the second time in four years. But the former champions somehow produced a brilliant display to stun the Dubliners 23-18, allowing long-time league leaders Clontarf to return to the summit by virtue of a 27-13 win over Ballynahinch.

Having been the bridesmaids so often, it was a massive relief for the club who celebrated in style a week later as the Barbarians visited Castle Avenue for a long-planned commemoration of the Battle of Clontarf that doubled up as an opportunity to rejoice in their success. 'We will take it any way we get it,' coach Andy Wood said of his side's last-gasp triumph. 'Thank goodness for Garryowen. We just knew that we had to win and hope that Garryowen would do us a favour. It wasn't the ideal situation but we also knew from our own experiences in recent weeks that anything could still happen.

'It's fantastic for this club that we have finally got our reward. We played well all season.'

There was some success for Munster clubs as Cork Constitution claimed the Ulster Bank Bateman Cup, with Darragh Lyons leading them to a final win over UCD at Temple Hill, but Garryowen's relegation saw them join Ireland's most successful club Shannon in Division 1B, and next season Limerick will only have one club – Young Munster – in the top flight.

BELOW Nenagh Ormond celebrate as Ulster Bank League Division 2B champions after beating Ards 29-7 to go through the programme unbeaten.

Ballynahinch survived relegation thanks to a play-off win over Buccaneers, while Terenure College return to Division 1A after winning the 1B title with a 100 per cent record.

Galwegians claimed the Division 2A title, while Nenagh Ormond won Division 2B as Kanturk and Wanderers won promotion to senior rugby through the Round Robin competition.

France: A Much Deeper Malaise? by CHRIS THAU

'Toulon won the Bouclier de Brennus for the first time this century, becoming the second French club to do the double of Heineken Cup and French Championship'

The 2014 French tour to Australia has concluded a rather modest season for Les Bleus, confirming a decline in fortunes which is reflected in the dry statistics of the IRB rankings. After the third consecutive defeat at the hands of the Wallabies, the thirteenth reverse in 19 matches, the French are seventh in the IRB rankings with a points average of 80.03, compared with their all-time high of 84.70 points in December 2011, after narrowly losing the RWC 2011 final. 'Given our results, this is a place which we probably deserve,' the French coach Philippe Saint-André said. The roots of the problem are complex, yet the ever increasing number of foreign players in the wealthy Top 14 league is perceived by many, including Saint-André, as one of the more visible causes of the problem.

ABOVE Jonny Wilkinson and the Toulon team with the Bouclier de Brennus after reversing the result of last year's Top 14 final by beating Castres Olympique at the Stade de France.

The French Federation regulations which allow a club like Toulon to field among their starting XV anything between 12 and 14 players who are not eligible to play for France should definitely come under scrutiny. If there is no strict regulation in professional sport, there is abuse. Interestingly, of the 26 Toulon players listed for the French Championship final against Castres Olympique only three or four were eligible to play for France. This is a fact, no matter what Toulon owner Mourad Boudjellal and his head coach Bernard Laporte might say. Mind you, Castres Olympique are not much better, though with about 24 foreign players out of a 38-strong squad they have more players eligible to play for France than their opponents.

By defeating Castres 18-10, with the retiring Jonny Wilkinson the author of 15 of his team's points tally, Toulon won the Bouclier de Brennus for the first time this century, becoming the second French club to do the double of Heineken Cup and French Championship after Toulouse in 1996. It was a dreary encounter in which the Toulon scrummage pounded the Castres eight into the ground, with the Castres and Scotland wing Max Evans the author of the game's only try. The Castres Olympique talisman, playmaker Rory Kockott, failed to produce the acts of magic of last year's final when he virtually single-handedly led his side to the championship gold medal. Last year he was supposed to have moved to Toulouse after the final, but it appeared that Castres made him an offer he could not refuse. Furthermore, it is widely speculated that the shortage of international-class talent in his position makes the South African-born scrum half a candidate for French international selection when he becomes eligible for France, probably this autumn.

BELOW One more time. Jonny Wilkinson, who retired after the match, brings that kicking style to bear on one of his four penalties in the Top 14 final. He also dropped a goal.

While Toulon parade their trophies to their adoring fans, traditional clubs of the likes of Toulouse, until recently the 'Koh-i-noor' of French club rugby, are punished for their commitment to develop French talent rather than buy overseas players. For the first time in 20 years Toulouse had missed the semi-finals of the French League, a clear sign

that, as head coach Guy Novès put it, 'enough is enough'. So what do they do after the final? They start looking abroad for new recruits. It is quite clear that it has become a disincentive to have too many players eligible to play for France in one's team. The more French players of the highest quality a club has got on its payroll, the more likely it is that it will suffer in the cut-throat domestic league (Top 14) when their stars are required for international action. Furthermore, a brutal touring schedule, which commences before the end of the domestic season and does not allow players involved in high-intensity rugby for several months any break, is also a contributing factor.

Unsurprisingly, in an interview in a leading French newspaper M Boudjellal rejected the allegations that foreign players are the cause of the decline in the fortunes of the French team in particular and French rugby in general. He is probably wrong. However, his claim that the real problem of French rugby is the elite development (the so-called Espoirs), which is not properly structured, managed and supervised, may have hit the nail on the head. This is the invisible aspect the journos, captivated by meaningless statistics, may have missed.

Interestingly, a recent decision of the FFR and the French League, which passed almost unnoticed by the media, was to limit the age of the players in the academy Espoirs system to 22 rather than 23, as it was until this season. The effect of this aberration was to make about 500 professional apprentices between the ages of 22 and 23 redundant while the clubs throughout the breadth of French rugby, Pro D2, Fédérale 1, Fédérale 2, Fédérale 3 etc, are busily employing young South Africans, Georgians, Kiwis, Irish, Welsh, English, Samoans, Tongans and Fijians.

Furthermore, the resources invested into development by less affluent clubs in the Top 14 and Pro D2 are pitiful, as the clubs, struggling to squeeze the extra Euro to pay their professional squads, are paying lip service to genuine investment in the future. There are a lot of talented and dedicated coaches working in the Espoirs structure of French professional rugby, but the selection and management of the youngsters is often left to fellow-travellers with little interest in and, more significantly, flair for development. Moreover, the head coaches of the professional sides in both the Top 14 and Pro D2, under pressure from their paymasters, would rather look abroad for quick fixes than allow their own talent to mature.

Once one of the most admired features of French rugby, that unique ability to let the ball do the talking while the players look for and find unique lines of running is now in short supply, while other nations work twice as hard on skill acquisition and development. The old adage 'practice makes perfect' was used to explain the outstanding skill set of some of the French players of the yesteryear generation of obsessive perfectionists of the likes of André and Guy Boniface, Jo Maso, Jean Trillo, Didier Codorniou, and Patrick Nadal in particular. Everything those compulsive artisans, who gave French rugby an almost mythical dimension, did was based on work – long hours of high-quality, intensive practice.

This is how the myth of French flair was born, defined as a capacity to produce magic moments of pure rugby skill out of almost anything – dour forward drives, brutal line-out contests and hard-fought scrums. In France now it remains an afterthought after the gym and track, where the hopefuls perfect their strength and speed, which can be measured. Skill cannot! The French backs coach Patrice Lagisquet, himself one of the finest purveyors of French flair, observed in an interview that the skill standard of French international players has dropped dramatically, forcing him to spend long hours fine-tuning aspects which in the past would have been part and parcel of the players' skill set.

In an essay published during the season, former France full back and coach Pierre Villepreux identified the short-term need to win as one of the barriers to progress, observing that continuity and pace in the game are based on a high-quality range of skills which are conspicuously absent. He noted also that the English and Celtic clubs, without the financial clout of the French, are able to produce a game which is more intense and ambitious than the one played by the French clubs.

'Since time immemorial European rugby, the national teams and therefore clubs have accepted modernity with reluctance, and therefore delay. The impulse to change the game came often from the Southern Hemisphere. The intensity of the game in today's Super 15 gives players more freedom of initiative. Within this framework and according to the game's culture, each country is able to reinvest its playing ambitions in their own national team. The matches between the two hemispheres highlight the backward spirit of old Europe,' he argued.

Italy: Calvisano Turn the Tables

by CHRIS THAU

'However, two yellow cards, a red card and two penalty tries, all in the second half and all against Rovigo, took the wind out of the visitors' sails, with Calvisano prevailing in the end'

Italy are finding life in the fast lane of professional rugby quite difficult, despite the visible progress they have made in both playing standards and elite development since joining the Six Nations in 2000. Their 26-23 defeat at the hands of Japan in the third match of the summer tour was their ninth consecutive defeat and those in the know feel that the relationship between the head coach Jacques Brunel and FIR President Alfredo Gavazzi has become distinctly frosty. Some say that the three-Test summer tour, with its unenviable record of three defeats out of three, was an unmitigated disaster, while some argue that Italy played quite well and ultimately winning the three-match tour was not necessarily the main objective of Brunel and his coaching team.

Furthermore, it was pointed out that Italy had been further weakened by the absence of skipper Sergio Parisse and prop Martin Castrogiovanni, whose presence could have made the difference in all three summer Tests.

The outcome of the first Test against Fiji was in the balance until the closing stages, with Fiji leading 18-14, when a converted try by Napolioni Nalaga in injury time gave the scoreline a rather distorted look at 25-14. Add to that two missed penalties, by the otherwise reliable Luciano Orquera, and the final score could have looked different. The Samoan Test was further proof that the Italian backs seem unable to score tries when it matters, though their defence held firm in the face of the Samoan onslaught.

BELOW The Calvisano driving maul about to lead to a penalty try in the Eccellenza final at the Peroni Stadium in Calvisano.

FACING PAGE Calvisano scrum half and captain Paul Griffen, who won 42 caps for Italy, retired after the final.

It is quite significant that after 20 years of professionalism there are only two professional players (Massimiliano Perziano and Brendan Williams) among the all-time top ten try scorers in domestic Italian rugby, with the legendary Marcello Cuttitta still leading the pack with 236 tries in five years (1985-90). This decline is decried by journalist Gianluca Barca in an editorial in his magazine *AllRugby*, pointing out that the inefficiency of the Italian game is widespread and is reflected in the performances of the various representative teams. 'It is quite indicative of this state of affairs that the top try-scorers in the Italian game are two hookers,' he wrote.

In Apia, captained by South African-born lock forward Quintin Geldenhuys the Italians battled bravely, but indiscipline cost them dearly as the Samoan outside half Tusi Pisi landed five penalties for a final scoreline of 15-0. With RWC 2015 looming large on the horizon, Brunel is making desperate efforts to develop the strength in depth of the Italian squad, which is arguably Italy's chief weakness. This is the objective of the Emerging Italy team, but their two defeats in this summer's Tbilisi Cup (the 45-20 loss to the Argentina Jaguars, and the 34-10 defeat by Georgia in particular) must have been ringing alarm bells at FIR headquarters in Rome. The only good news came unexpectedly on 20 September 2013, when both professional outfits, Benetton Treviso and Zebre, managed to register two rare wins against previously unbeaten opponents in the RaboDirect PRO12: Treviso beat Munster 29-19, while Zebre had the better of Cardiff Blues 30-25 at Cardiff Arms Park.

On the club scene, at the end of the regular domestic season, Calvisano, coached by Gianluca Guidi, a former coach of Emerging Italy, were top of the table with 88 points followed by Rovigo, experiencing a revival after several years in the doldrums, with 83, Mogliano with 63 and Viadana with 61. In the play-offs Calvisano emphatically defeated Viadana, winning both legs (30-19 and 65-14), while Rovigo managed to knock out Mogliano (22-19 and 31-30). It is worth remembering that Rovigo coaches Andrea de Rossi and Filippo Frati, who joined the club at the end of the previous season from Estra I Cavalieri Prato, had managed to bring with them from their previous club no less than ten regulars. No surprise therefore that I Cavalieri, after playing in the final last year, finished the league in sixth position. The final itself between Cammi Calvisano and Vea Femi-CZ Rovigo was a bizarre affair, which generated a fair amount of controversy. Within ten minutes, Rovigo had scored two converted tries and a penalty to take the lead by 17 points to nil. Calvisano's New Zealand-born outside half Kelly Haimona landed the first of his three first-half penalties in the 14th minute, Rovigo leading 17-9 at the break. However, two yellow cards, a red card and two penalty tries, all in the second half and all against Rovigo, took the wind out of the visitors' sails, with Calvisano prevailing in the end 26-17, to win their third championship title since 2000. This was also the last match for New Zealand-born Calvisano and Italy scrum half Paul Griffen, who announced his retirement from the game.

A Summary of the Season 2013-14

by TERRY COOPER

INTERNATIONAL RUGBY

AUSTRALIA TO EUROPE, NOVEMBER 2013

Opponents	Results
ENGLAND	L 13-20
ITALY	W 50-20
IRELAND	W 32-15
SCOTLAND	W 21-15
WALES	W 30-26

Played 5 Won 4 Lost 1

SOUTH AFRICA TO EUROPE, NOVEMBER 2013

Opponents	Results
WALES	W 24-15
SCOTLAND	W 28-0
FRANCE	W 19-10

Played 3 Won 3

NEW ZEALAND TO JAPAN & EUROPE, NOVEMBER/DECEMBER 2013

Opponents	Results
JAPAN	W 54-6
FRANCE	W 26-19
ENGLAND	W 30-22
IRELAND	W 24-22

Played 4 Won 4

ARGENTINA TO EUROPE, NOVEMBER 2013

Opponents	Results
ENGLAND	L 12-31
WALES	L 6-40
ITALY	W 19-14

Played 3 Won 1 Lost 2

TONGA TO EUROPE, NOVEMBER 2013

Opponents	Results
ROMANIA	L 18-19
FRANCE	L 18-38
WALES	L 7-17

Played 3 Lost 3

FIJI TO EUROPE, NOVEMBER 2013

Opponents	Results
PORTUGAL	W 36-13
ITALY	L 31-37
ROMANIA	W 26-7
Barbarians	L 19-43

Played 4 Won 2 Lost 2

SAMOA TO EUROPE NOVEMBER 2013

Opponents	Results
IRELAND	L 9-40
French Barbarians	L 19-20
GEORGIA	L 15-16

Played 3 Lost 3

JAPAN TO EUROPE, NOVEMBER 2013

Opponents	Results
SCOTLAND	L 17-42
Gloucester	L 5-40
RUSSIA	W 40-13
SPAIN	W 40-7

Played 4 Won 2 Lost 2

ENGLAND TO NEW ZEALAND, JUNE 2014

Opponents	Results
NEW ZEALAND	L 15-20
NEW ZEALAND	L 27-28
Crusaders	W 38-7
NEW ZEALAND	L 13-36

Played 4 Won 1 Lost 3

SCOTLAND TO THE AMERICAS & SOUTH AFRICA, JUNE 2014

Opponents	Results
USA	W 24-6
CANADA	W 19-17
ARGENTINA	W 21-19
SOUTH AFRICA	L 6-55

Played 4 Won 3 Lost 1

IRELAND TO ARGENTINA, JUNE 2014

Opponents	Results
ARGENTINA	W 29–17
ARGENTINA	W 23–17

Played 2 Won 2

WALES TO SOUTH AFRICA, JUNE 2014

Opponents	Results
Eastern Kings	W 34-12
SOUTH AFRICA	L 16-38
SOUTH AFRICA	L 30-31

Played 3 Won 1 Lost 2

FRANCE TO AUSTRALIA, JUNE 2014

Opponents	Results
AUSTRALIA	L 23-50
AUSTRALIA	L 0-6
AUSTRALIA	L 13-39

Played 3 Lost 3

ITALY TO THE SOUTH PACIFIC & JAPAN, JUNE 2014

Opponents	Results
FIJI	L 14-25
SAMOA	L 0 15
JAPAN	L 23-26

Played 3 Lost 3

ROYAL BANK OF SCOTLAND 6 NATIONS CHAMPIONSHIP 2014

Results

Wales	23	Italy	15
France	26	England	24
Ireland	28	Scotland	6
Ireland	26	Wales	3
Scotland	0	England	20
France	30	Italy	10
Wales	27	France	6
Italy	20	Scotland	21
England	13	Ireland	10
Ireland	46	Italy	7
Scotland	17	France	19
England	29	Wales	18
Italy	11	England	52
Wales	51	Scotland	3
France	20	Ireland	22

Final Table

	P	W	D	L	F	A	PD	Pts
Ireland	5	4	0	1	132	49	83	8
England	5	4	0	1	138	65	73	8
Wales	5	3	0	2	122	79	43	6
France	5	3	0	2	101	100	1	6
Scotland	5	1	0	4	47	138	-91	2
Italy	5	0	0	5	63	172	-109	0

UNDER 20 SIX NATIONS 2014

Results

Ireland	34	Scotland	7
Wales	26	Italy	9
France	21	England	15
Scotland	15	England	48
Ireland	0	Wales	16
France	34	Italy	0
Italy	32	Scotland	13
Wales	10	France	16
England	33	Ireland	9
Ireland	18	Italy	0
Scotland	13	France	18
England	67	Wales	7
Italy	5	England	52
Wales	43	Scotland	15
France	23	Ireland	13

Final Table

	P	W	D	L	F	A	PD	Pts
France	5	5	0	0	112	51	61	10
England	5	4	0	1	215	57	158	8
Wales	5	3	0	2	102	107	-5	6
Ireland	5	2	0	3	74	79	-5	4
Italy	5	1	0	4	46	143	-97	2
Scotland	5	0	0	5	63	175	-112	0

IRB PACIFIC NATIONS CUP 2014

(Held in June)

Samoa	18	Tonga	18
Canada	25	Japan	34
Fiji	45	Tonga	17
USA	29	Japan	37
Fiji	13	Samoa	18
USA	38	Canada	35

Group Winners
North America: Japan
Pacific: Samoa

IRB NATIONS CUP 2014

(Held in June in Bucharest, Romania)

Emerging Ireland	66	Russia	0
Romania	34	Uruguay	16
Emerging Ireland	51	Uruguay	3
Romania	20	Russia	18
Russia	6	Uruguay	13
Romania	10	Emerging Ireland	31

Champions: Emerging Ireland
Runners-up: Romania

IRB JUNIOR WORLD CHAMPIONSHIP 2014

(Held in June in New Zealand)

Semi-finals

England	42	Ireland	15
South Africa	32	New Zealand	25

Third-place Play-off

Ireland	23	New Zealand	45

Final

England	21	South Africa	20

IRB JUNIOR WORLD RUGBY TROPHY 2014

(Held in April in Hong Kong)

Third-place Play-off
USA	26	Uruguay	25

Final
Tonga	10	Japan	35

FIRA/AER EUROPEAN UNDER 18 CHAMPIONSHIP 2014 – ELITE DIVISION

(Held in April in Poland)

Semi-finals
England	11	Wales	9
France	11	Ireland	24

Third-place Play-off
Wales	31	France	30

Final
England	30	Ireland	14

THE RUGBY CHAMPIONSHIP 2013

Results
Australia	29	New Zealand	47
South Africa	73	Argentina	13
New Zealand	27	Australia	16
Argentina	17	South Africa	22
New Zealand	28	Argentina	13
Australia	12	South Africa	38
New Zealand	29	South Africa	15
Australia	14	Argentina	13
South Africa	28	Australia	8
Argentina	15	New Zealand	33
South Africa	27	New Zealand	38
Argentina	17	Australia	54

Final Table
	P	W	D	L	PD	BP	Pts
New Zealand	6	6	0	0	87	4	28
South Africa	6	4	0	2	86	3	19
Australia	6	2	0	4	-37	1	9
Argentina	6	0	0	6	-136	2	2

HSBC SEVENS WORLD SERIES FINALS 2013-14

Australia (Gold Coast)
New Zealand	40	Australia	19

Dubai
Fiji	29	South Africa	17

South Africa (Port Elizabeth)
New Zealand	14	South Africa	17

USA (Las Vegas)
South Africa	14	New Zealand	7

New Zealand (Wellington)
New Zealand	21	South Africa	0

Japan (Tokyo)
Fiji	33	South Africa	26

Hong Kong
England	7	New Zealand	26

Scotland (Glasgow)
New Zealand	54	Canada	7

England (Twickenham)
Australia	33	New Zealand	52

Champions: New Zealand

COMMONWEALTH GAMES 2014 RUGBY SEVENS TOURNAMENT

(Held in July in Glasgow)

Shield Final
Trinidad & Tobago	7	Sri Lanka	43

Bowl Final
Canada	50	Cook Islands	7

Plate Final
Wales	15	England	17

Bronze Medal Match
Australia	24	Samoa	0

Gold Medal Match
New Zealand	12	South Africa	17

WOMEN'S SIX NATIONS 2014

Results
Ireland	59	Scotland	0
France	18	England	6
Wales	11	Italy	12
Ireland	14	Wales	6
France	29	Italy	0
Scotland	0	England	63
England	17	Ireland	10
Wales	0	France	27
Italy	45	Scotland	5
England	35	Wales	3
Ireland	39	Italy	0
Scotland	0	France	69
France	19	Ireland	15
Wales	25	Scotland	0
Italy	0	England	24

Final Table
	P	W	D	L	F	A	PD	Pts
France	5	5	0	0	162	21	141	10
England	5	4	0	1	145	31	114	8
Ireland	5	3	0	2	137	42	95	6
Italy	5	2	0	3	57	108	-51	4
Wales	5	1	0	4	45	88	-43	2
Scotland	5	0	0	5	5	261	-256	0

FACING PAGE Scenes from the Commonwealth Games 2014 Rugby Sevens tournament, which took place at Ibrox Stadium, Glasgow, on 26-27 July. Clockwise from left: Emma Ecodu of Uganda after scoring against Australia; Trinidad & Tobago v Cook Islands; Malaysia v Papua New Guinea; Cecil Afrika scores for South Africa against New Zealand in the Gold Medal Match.

CLUB, COUNTY AND DIVISIONAL RUGBY

ENGLAND

Aviva Premiership

	P	W	D	L	F	A	BP	Pts
Saracens	22	19	0	3	629	353	11	87
Northampton	22	16	2	4	604	350	10	78
Leicester	22	15	2	5	542	430	10	74
Harlequins	22	15	0	7	437	365	7	67
Bath	22	14	2	6	495	388	7	67
Sale	22	12	0	10	432	399	9	57
Wasps	22	9	0	13	451	533	13	49
Exeter	22	9	0	13	426	480	9	45
Gloucester	22	8	0	14	440	539	12	44
London Irish	22	7	0	15	396	496	8	36
Newcastle	22	3	0	19	281	544	10	22
Worcester	22	2	0	20	325	581	8	16

Relegated: Worcester

Aviva Premiership Play-offs
Semi-finals

Northampton	21	Leicester	20
Saracens	31	Harlequins	27

Final

Saracens	20	Northampton	24

Greene King IPA Championship Play-offs
Semi-finals (1st leg)

Bristol	17	Rotherham Titans	14
Leeds Carnegie	38	London Welsh	31

Semi-finals (2nd leg)

Rotherham Titans	11	Bristol	22
London Welsh	29	Leeds Carnegie	20

Final

London Welsh	27	Bristol	8
Bristol	20	London Welsh	21

Promoted to Premiership: London Welsh

National Leagues
National 1 Champions: Doncaster Knights
Runners-up: Rosslyn Park
National 2 (S) Champions: Hartpury College
Runners-up: Ampthill
National 2 (N) Champions: Macclesfield
Runners-up: Darlington Mowden Park

National 2 N & S Runners-up Play-off

Darlington M'den Pk	30	Ampthill	28

RFU Knockout Trophy Finals
Intermediate Cup

Trowbridge	22	Leek	19

Senior Vase

Newent	20	Yarnbury	13

Junior Vase

Longlevens	23	Rugby Lions	12

County Championships
Bill Beaumont Cup Division One Final

Lancashire	36	Cornwall	26

County Championship Division 2 Plate Final

Kent	31	Durham	23

County Championship Shield Final

Surrey	39	Leicestershire	16

National Under 20 Championship Final

Yorkshire	10	Northumberland	39

National Under 17 Cup Final

Wolverhampton	7	Sevenoaks	3

Oxbridge University Matches
Varsity Match

Oxford	33	Cambridge	15

Under 21 Varsity Match

Oxford	19	Cambridge	30

Women's Varsity Match

Oxford	17	Cambridge	12

BUCS Competitions
Men's Championship Winners: UWE Hartpury
Women's Championship Winners: Cardiff Met

Inter-Service Championship

Royal Navy	10	Royal Air Force	0
Royal Air Force	26	Army	35
Army	30	Royal Navy	17

Champions: Army

Hospitals Cup Winners: Imperial Medics

Rosslyn Park Schools Sevens
Open Winners: Millfield School
Festival Winners: Bedford School
Colts Winners: QEGS Wakefield
Preparatory Winners: Millfield Preparatory School
Juniors Winners: RGS High Wycombe
Girls Winners: Clyst Vale Community College

NatWest Schools Cup Finals Day
Under 18 Cup Winners: Dulwich College
Under 18 Vase Winners: Trent College
Under 15 Cup Winners: Warwick School
Under 15 Vase Winners: Altrincham GS

Women's Premiership

	P	W	D	L	F	A	BP	Pts
Richmond	14	13	0	1	599	127	11	63
Saracens	14	12	1	1	449	112	12	62
Bristol	14	8	2	4	364	244	6	42
Worcester	14	7	2	5	381	235	6	38
Darlington MP	14	6	1	7	239	298	5	31
Lichfield	14	3	0	11	278	349	7	19
Wasps	14	3	0	11	144	402	4	16
Aylesford Bulls	14	1	0	13	71	758	1	5

SCOTLAND

RBS Cup
Semi-finals

Gala	31	Glasgow Hawks	33
Aberdeen GS	16	Heriot's	20

Final

Glasgow Hawks	10	Heriot's	31

RBS Shield Final
Caithness	6	Preston Lodge	27

RBS Bowl Final
Highland	26	Glenrothes	12

Scottish Sevens Winners
Kelso: Melrose
Selkirk: Melrose
Melrose: Glasgow Warriors
Hawick: Melrose
Berwick: Gala
Langholm: Melrose
Peebles: Melrose
Gala: Melrose
Earlston: Melrose
Jed-Forest: Melrose
Kings of the Sevens: Melrose

RBS Premiership
	P	W	D	L	F	A	BP	Pts
Melrose	18	15	0	3	494	312	9	69
Gala	18	13	1	4	481	315	14	66
Ayr	18	13	0	5	456	294	13	65
Heriot's	18	12	1	5	403	347	8	58
Glasgow Hawks	18	6	2	10	392	416	9	37
Hawick	18	6	1	11	354	449	8	34
Currie	18	7	1	10	357	464	4	34
Stirling County	18	6	0	12	278	358	9	33
Edinburgh Accies	18	6	0	12	339	485	7	31
Aberdeen GS	18	3	0	15	338	452	11	23

RBS Premiership Play-off
Edinburgh Accies	23	Stewart's Melville	13

RBS National League
	P	W	D	L	F	A	BP	Pts
Boroughmuir	18	16	0	2	591	246	14	78
Stewart's Melville	18	13	1	4	381	293	9	63
Watsonians	18	12	0	6	592	319	14	62
Dundee HSFP	18	12	1	5	499	303	9	59
Selkirk	18	10	1	7	503	349	12	54
Kelso	18	10	1	7	411	454	9	51
Peebles	18	6	1	11	339	399	6	32
GHA	18	4	0	14	298	581	6	22
Hillhead J'hill	18	3	0	15	272	558	7	19
Biggar	18	1	1	16	230	614	3	9

RBS Women's Premier League
Champions: Hillhead Jordanhill

Sarah Beaney Cup
Winners: Murrayfield Wanderers

WALES

SWALEC Cup
Semi-finals

Aberavon	3	Pontypridd	32
Cross Keys	29	Llandovery	27

Final

Pontypridd	21	Cross Keys	8

SWALEC Plate Final
Merthyr	29	Rhiwbina	26

SWALEC Bowl Final
Llantwit Major	10	CRCC	16

Principality Premiership
	P	W	D	L	F	A	BP	Pts
Pontypridd	22	16	1	5	646	465	12	78
Carmarthen	22	18	0	4	501	374	5	77
Cross Keys	22	14	0	8	483	362	13	69
Llandovery	22	13	3	6	554	413	11	69
Llanelli	22	13	1	8	567	500	11	65
Bedwas	22	11	0	11	450	498	9	53
Cardiff	22	10	0	12	430	523	7	47
Newport	22	8	1	13	483	520	9	43
Bridgend	22	7	1	14	470	547	12	42
Aberavon	22	7	1	14	330	510	3	33
Neath	22	6	0	16	437	536	9	33
Swansea	22	5	0	17	421	524	12	32

SWALEC Championship
	P	W	D	L	F	A	BP	Pts
Ebbw Vale	26	25	0	1	1009	221	22	122
Cardiff Met	26	17	1	8	716	487	16	86
RGC 1404	26	17	0	9	743	419	15	83
Pontypool	26	17	1	8	644	463	13	83
Narberth	26	16	2	8	656	469	12	80
Bargoed	26	15	0	11	562	435	14	74
Tata Steel	26	13	0	13	559	561	13	65
Bridgend Ath	26	13	1	12	478	557	6	60
Tondu	26	11	0	15	431	637	9	53
Llanharan	26	10	0	16	471	678	8	48
Blackwood	26	6	1	19	505	773	13	39
Newbridge	26	7	1	18	349	610	8	38
Beddau	26	5	2	19	378	734	6	30
Bonymaen	26	5	1	20	294	753	5	27

SWALEC Leagues
Division 1 East Champions: Merthyr
Division 1 North Champions: Bala
Division 1 West Champions: Glynneath

Women's Super Cup Finals
Cup Final

Neath Athletic	36	Pontyclun Falcons	16

Plate Final

Seven Sisters	15	Pencoed	13

Bowl Final

Kidwelly	34	Maesteg Celtic	31

Vase Final

Penybanc	33	Haverfordwest	5

IRELAND

Ulster Bank League Division 1A

	P	W	D	L	F	A	BP	Pts
Clontarf	18	14	0	4	485	279	8	64
Old Belvedere	18	13	2	3	377	299	7	63
UCD	18	10	0	8	433	386	7	47
Lansdowne	18	9	0	9	428	387	11	47
Cork Const'n	18	8	2	8	296	315	9	45
St Mary's College	18	8	2	8	384	370	8	44
Young Munster	18	8	0	10	321	399	5	37
Dolphin	18	8	0	10	259	385	5	37
Ballynahinch	18	5	0	13	337	356	12	32
Garryowen	18	4	0	14	251	395	6	22

Ulster Bank League Division 1B

	P	W	D	L	F	A	BP	Pts
Terenure College	18	18	0	0	514	210	10	82
Buccaneers	18	12	0	6	440	326	11	59
UL Bohemian	18	10	0	8	360	325	12	52
Corinthians	18	12	0	6	340	327	4	52
Shannon	18	9	0	9	286	329	5	41
Belfast H'quins	18	8	0	10	312	305	6	38
Dublin University	18	7	0	11	286	319	9	37
Malone	18	6	0	12	351	365	11	35
Blackrock College	18	5	1	12	350	441	9	31
Dungannon	18	2	1	15	251	543	3	13

Ulster Bank League Division 2A
Champions: Galwegians

Ulster Bank League Division 2B
Champions: Nenagh Ormond

Round Robin
OLBC	7	Kanturk	13
Wanderers	21	Clogher Valley	7
Clogher Valley	27	OLBC	11
Kanturk	29	Wanderers	30
Kanturk	18	Clogher Valley	7
Wanderers	51	OLBC	7

Winners: Wanderers

All Ireland Cup Final
Cork Constitution	19	UCD	6

All Ireland Junior Cup Final
Clogher Valley	9	Enniscorthy	10

Fraser McMullen Under 21 Cup Final
Cork Constitution	12	Terenure	7

RABODIRECT PRO12 2013-14

	P	W	D	L	F	A	BP	Pts
Leinster	22	17	1	4	554	352	12	82
Warriors	22	18	0	4	484	309	7	79
Munster	22	16	0	6	538	339	10	74
Ulster	22	15	0	7	470	319	10	70
Ospreys	22	13	1	8	571	388	12	66
Scarlets	22	11	1	10	435	438	9	55
Blues	22	8	1	13	425	538	7	41
Edinburgh	22	7	0	15	397	526	10	38
Dragons	22	7	1	14	392	492	5	35
Connacht	22	6	0	16	371	509	11	35
Treviso	22	5	1	16	376	591	8	30
Zebre	22	5	2	15	347	559	5	29

RaboDirect PRO12 Play-offs
Semi-finals
Warriors	16	Munster	15
Leinster	13	Ulster	9

Final
Leinster	34	Warriors	12

LV= CUP 2013-14

Semi-finals
Northampton	26	Saracens	7
Bath	19	Exeter	22

Final
Exeter	15	Northampton	8

BRITISH & IRISH CUP 2013-14

Final
Leinster A	44	Leeds Carnegie	17

FRANCE

'Top 14' Play-offs
Semi-finals
Montpellier	19	Castres	22
Toulon	16	Racing Métro 92	6

Final
Toulon	18	Castres	10

ITALY

Campionato Nazionale Eccellenza

Final
Calvisano   26   Rovigo   17

HEINEKEN CUP 2013-14

Quarter-finals
Munster   47   Toulouse   23
Clermont Auvergne   22   Leicester   16
Ulster   15   Saracens   17
Toulon   29   Leinster   14

Semi-finals
Saracens   46   Clermont Auvergne   6
Toulon   24   Munster   16

Final
Toulon   23   Saracens   6

AMLIN CHALLENGE CUP 2013-14

Quarter-finals
Sale   14   Northampton   28
Stade Français   6   Harlequins   29
Bath   39   Brive   7
Wasps   36   Gloucester   24

Semi-finals
Northampton   18   Harlequins   10
Wasps   18   Bath   24

Final
Bath   16   Northampton   30

NEW ZEALAND

ITM Cup Premiership Final 2013

Wellington   13   Canterbury   29

ITM Cup Championship Final 2013

Tasman   26   Hawke's Bay   25

Heartland Champions 2013
Meads Cup: Mid Canterbury
Lochore Cup: South Canterbury

Ranfurly Shield holders: Counties Manukau

SOUTH AFRICA

Currie Cup 2013

Final
Sharks   33   Western Province 19

SUPER RUGBY 2014

	P	W	D	L	F	A	BP	Pts
Waratahs	16	12	0	4	481	272	10	58
Crusaders	16	11	0	5	445	322	7	51
Sharks	16	11	0	5	406	293	6	50
Brumbies	16	10	0	6	412	378	5	45
Chiefs	16	8	2	6	384	378	8	44
Highlanders	16	8	0	8	401	442	10	42
Hurricanes	16	8	0	8	439	374	9	41
Force	16	9	0	7	343	393	4	40
Bulls	16	7	1	8	365	335	6	38
Blues	16	7	0	9	419	395	9	37
Stormers	16	7	0	9	290	326	4	32
Lions	16	7	0	9	367	413	3	31
Reds	16	5	0	11	374	493	8	28
Cheetahs	16	4	1	11	372	527	6	24
Rebels	16	4	0	12	303	460	5	21

Qualifiers
Brumbies   32   Chiefs   30
Sharks   31   Highlanders   27

Semi-finals
Crusaders   38   Sharks   6
Waratahs   26   Brumbies   8

Final
Waratahs   33   Crusaders   32

Key
Waratahs: Conference leaders
Brumbies: Wild Card teams

Note: The top two Conference leaders – Waratahs and Crusaders – received a bye to the semi-finals

BARBARIANS

Opponents	Results
Combined Services	L 28-34
Fiji XV	W 43-19
Clontarf	L 42-43
England XV	W 39-29

Played 4 Won 2 Lost 2

PREVIEW OF THE
SEASON 2014-15

Key Players
selected by IAN ROBERTSON

ENGLAND

LUTHER BURRELL
Northampton Saints
Born: 6 December 1987
Height: 6ft 3ins Weight: 17st 2lbs
Centre – 7 caps
1st cap v France 2014

BILLY VUNIPOLA
Saracens
Born: 3 November 1992
Height: 6ft 2ins Weight: 19st 11lbs
Back-row – 10 caps
1st cap v Argentina 2013

SCOTLAND

FINN RUSSELL
Glasgow Warriors
Born: 23 September 1992
Height: 6ft Weight: 12st 8lbs
Fly half – 2 caps
1st cap v USA 2014

JONNY GRAY
Glasgow Warriors
Born: 14 March 1994
Height: 6ft 6ins Weight: 19st
Lock – 5 caps
1st cap v South Africa 2013

WALES

ALEX CUTHBERT
Blues
Born: 5 April 1990
Height: 6ft 6ins Weight: 16st 9lbs
Wing – 26 caps (+1 Lions)
1st cap v Australia 2011

RICHARD HIBBARD
Gloucester
Born: 13 December 1983
Height: 6ft Weight: 17st 4lbs
Hooker – 31 caps (+3 Lions)
1st cap v Argentina 2006

Six Nations Championship
2014-15

IRELAND

IAN MADIGAN
Leinster
Born: 21 March 1989
Height: 5ft 11ins Weight: 14st 2lbs
Fly half – 10 caps
1st cap v France 2013

CHRIS HENRY
Ulster
Born: 17 October 1984
Height: 6ft 3ins Weight: 16st 11lbs
Back-row – 16 caps
1st cap v Australia 2010

FRANCE

MATHIEU BASTAREAUD
Toulon
Born: 17 September 1988
Height: 6ft Weight: 17st 6lbs
Centre – 25 caps
1st cap v Wales 2009

DIMITRI SZARZEWSKI
Racing Métro 92
Born: 26 January 1983
Height: 5ft 11ins Weight: 16st
Hooker – 79 caps
1st cap v Canada 2004

ITALY

LUCIANO ORQUERA
Zebre
Born: 12 October 1981
Height: 5ft 7ins Weight: 12st 6lbs
Fly half – 44 caps
1st cap v Canada 2004

ROBERT BARBIERI
Treviso
Born: 5 June 1984
Height: 6ft 1in Weight: 17st
Back-row – 37 caps
1st cap v Japan 2006

Fixtures 2014-15

AUGUST 2014

Sat. 16th	AUSTRALIA v NZ (TRC)
	SA v ARGENTINA (TRC)
Sat. 16th and	
Sun. 17th	World Club 7s (Twickenham)
Sat. 23rd	NZ v AUSTRALIA (TRC))
	ARGENTINA v SA (TRC)
Sat. 30th	BT Scottish Premiership
	BT Scottish Cup (1)

SEPTEMBER 2014

Fri. 5th to	
Sun. 7th	Aviva English Premiership (1)
	Greene King IPA Championship
	Guinness PRO12 (1)
Sat. 6th	AUSTRALIA v SA (TRC)
	NZ v ARGENTINA (TRC)
	English National Leagues
	BT Scottish Premiership
	BT Scottish National Leagues
	Swalec Welsh Nat Ch/ship
	Swalec Welsh National Lges
Mon. 8th	Aviva 'A' League (1)
Fri. 12th and	
Sat. 13th	Ulster Bank Irish Leagues
Fri. 12th to	
Sun. 14th	Aviva English Premiership (2)
	Guinness PRO12 (2)
Sat. 13th	AUSTRALIA v ARGENTINA (TRC)
	NZ v SA (TRC)
	English National Leagues
	BT Scottish Premiership
	BT Scottish National Leagues
	Welsh Principality Pr/ship (1)
	Swalec Welsh Nat Ch/ship
	Swalec Welsh National Lges
Sat. 13th and	
Sun. 14th	Greene King IPA Championship
Mon. 15th	Aviva 'A' League (2)
Fri. 19th to	
Sun. 21st	Aviva English Premiership (3)
	Greene King IPA Championship
	Guinness PRO12 (3)
Sat. 20th	English National Leagues
	BT Scottish Premiership
	BT Scottish National Leagues
	Welsh Principality Pr/ship (2)
	Swalec Welsh Nat Ch/ship
	Swalec Welsh National Lges
	Ulster Bank Irish Leagues
Mon. 22nd	Aviva 'A' League (3)
Fri. 26th and	
Sat. 27th	Ulster Bank Irish Leagues
Fri. 26th to	
Sun. 28th	Aviva English Premiership (4)
	Greene King IPA Championship
	Guinness PRO12 (4)
Sat. 27th	SA v AUSTRALIA (TRC)

	ARGENTINA v NZ (TRC)
	English National Leagues
	BT Scottish Premiership
	BT Scottish National Leagues
	Welsh Principality Pr/ship (3)
	Swalec Welsh Nat Ch/ship
	Swalec Welsh Plate (1)

OCTOBER 2014

Fri. 3rd and	
Sat. 4th	Ulster Bank Irish Leagues
Fri. 3rd to	
Sun. 5th	Aviva English Premiership (5)
	Guinness PRO12 (5)
Sat. 4th	SA v NZ (TRC)
	ARGENTINA v AUSTRALIA (TRC)
	Greene King IPA Championship
	English National Leagues
	BT Scottish Premiership
	BT Scottish National Leagues
	Welsh Principality Pr/ship (4)
	Swalec Welsh Nat Ch/ship
	Swalec Welsh National Lges
Mon. 6th	Aviva 'A' League (4)
Fri. 10th to	
Sun. 12th	Aviva English Premiership (6)
	Guinness PRO12 (6)
Sat. 11th	English National Leagues
	BT Scottish Premiership
	BT Scottish National Leagues
	Swalec Welsh Nat Ch/ship
	Swalec Welsh National Lges
Sat. 11th and	
Sun.12th	British & Irish Cup (1)
Mon. 13th	Aviva 'A' League (5)
Thu. 16th to	
Sun. 19th	European Champions Cup (1)
	European Challenge Cup (1)
Sat. 18th	English National Leagues
	British & Irish Cup (2)
	BT Scottish Premiership
	BT Scottish National Leagues
	Swalec Welsh Nat Ch/ship
	Swalec Welsh National Lges
Thu. 23rd to	
Sun. 26th	European Champions Cup (2)
	European Challenge Cup (2)
Sat. 25th	English National Leagues
	British & Irish Cup (3)
	BT Scottish Premiership
	BT Scottish National Leagues
	Swalec Welsh Nat Ch/ship
	Swalec Welsh Plate (2)

NOVEMBER 2014

Fri. 31st Oct.	
and Sat. 1st	LV= (Anglo-Welsh) Cup (1)
	Ulster Bank Irish Leagues

Fri. 31st Oct.
to Sun. 2nd   Guinness PRO12 (7)
Sat. 1st   Barbarians v Australia
                     (Killik Cup)
                 USA v NEW ZEALAND
                 English National Leagues
                 BT Scottish Premiership
                 BT Scottish National Leagues
                 Welsh Principality Pr/ship (5)
                 Swalec Welsh Nat Ch/ship
                 Swalec Welsh National Lges

Fri. 7th and
Sat. 8th   BT Scottish National Leagues
                 Ulster Bank Irish Leagues

Fri. 7th or
Sun. 9th   Welsh Principality Pr/ship (6)
Fri. 7th to
Sun. 9th   Greene King IPA Championship
                 LV= (Anglo-Welsh) Cup (2)
Sat. 8th   ENGLAND v NZ
                 IRELAND v SA
                 SCOTLAND v ARGENTINA
                 ITALY v SAMOA
                 English National Leagues 1, 2
                 National U20 Shield (1)
Fri. 14th   WALES v FIJI
Fri. 14th or
Sun. 16th   Welsh Principality Pr/ship (7)
Fri. 14th and
Sat. 15th   Greene King IPA Championship
                 Ulster Bank Irish Leagues
Sat. 15th   ENGLAND v SA
                 SCOTLAND v NZ
                 IRELAND v GEORGIA
                 ITALY v ARGENTINA
                 FRANCE v AUSTRALIA
                 English National Leagues
                 BT Scottish Cup (2)

Sat. 15th and
Sun. 16th   Aviva English Premiership (7)
Fri. 21st or
Sun. 23rd   Welsh Principality Pr/ship (8)
Fri. 21st to
Sun. 23rd   Aviva English Premiership (8)
                 Greene King IPA Championship
                 Guinness PRO12 (8)
Sat. 22nd   ENGLAND v SAMOA
                 WALES v NZ
                 IRELAND v AUSTRALIA
                 FRANCE v ARGENTINA
                 SCOTLAND v TONGA
                 ITALY v SA
                 English National Leagues

Sat. 22nd and
Sun. 23rd   Ulster Bank Irish Leagues
Fri. 28th and
Sat. 29th   British & Irish Cup (4)
Fri. 28th to
Sun. 30th   Guinness PRO12 (9)
Sat. 29th   ENGLAND v AUSTRALIA
                 WALES v SA
                 English National Leagues 1, 2

                 National U20 Ch/ship (1)
                 National U20 Shield (2)
                 BT Scottish Premiership
                 BT Scottish National Leagues
Sat. 29th and
Sun. 30th   Aviva English Premiership (9)

DECEMBER 2014

Thu. 4th to
Sun. 7th   European Champions Cup (3)
                 European Challenge Cup (3)
Sat. 6th   English National Leagues
                 BT Scottish Premiership
                 BT Scottish National Leagues
                 Swalec Welsh Nat Ch/ship
                 Swalec Welsh National Lges

Sat. 6th and
Sun. 7th   British & Irish Cup (5)
                 Ulster Bank Irish Leagues
Thu. 11th   Oxford U v Cambridge U
                 OU U21 v CU U21
Thu. 11th to
Sun. 14th   European Champions Cup (4)
                 European Challenge Cup (4)
Sat. 13th   English National Leagues
                 British & Irish Cup (6)
                 BT Scottish Premiership
                 BT Scottish National Leagues
                 Swalec Welsh Nat Ch/ship
                 Swalec Welsh Plate (3)
Mon. 15th   Aviva 'A' League (6)
Fri. 19th and
Sat. 20th   Ulster Bank Irish Leagues
Fri. 19th to
Sun. 21st   Guinness PRO12 (10)
Sat. 20th   Aviva English Premiership (10)
                 Greene King IPA Championship
                 English National Leagues
                 BT Scottish National Leagues
                 Welsh Principality Pr/ship (9)
                 Swalec Welsh Nat Ch/ship
                 Swalec Welsh National Lges
Mon. 22nd   Aviva 'A' League (7)
Fri. 26th and
Sat. 27th   Aviva English Premiership (11)
                 Greene King IPA Championship
                 Welsh Principality Pr/ship (10)
Fri. 26th to
Sun. 28th   Guinness PRO12 (11)
Sat. 27th   Swalec Welsh Nat Ch/ship

JANUARY 2015

Thu. 1st   Greene King IPA Championship
Fri. 2nd and
Sat. 3rd   Ulster Bank Irish Leagues
Fri. 2nd to
Sun. 4th   Guinness PRO12 (12)
Sat. 3rd   Greene King IPA Championship
                 English National Leagues
                 National U20 Ch/ship (2)
                 National U20 Shield (3)
                 BT Scottish Cup (3)

Sat. 3rd and Sun. 4th	Welsh Principality Pr/ship (11) Swalec Welsh Nat Ch/ship Swalec Welsh National Lges	Fri. 13th to Sun. 15th	Swalec Welsh National Lges Greene King IPA Championship Welsh Principality Pr/ship (16)
Fri. 9th to Sun. 11th	Aviva English Premiership (12)	Sat. 14th	Guinness PRO12 (14) ENGLAND v ITALY (14:30)
Sat. 10th	Guinness PRO12 (13) Greene King IPA Championship English National Leagues BT Scottish Premiership BT Scottish National Leagues Swalec Welsh National Lges Swalec Welsh Cup (1) Ulster Bank Irish Leagues		IRELAND v FRANCE (17:00) RBS U20 Six Nations English National Leagues 1, 2 National U20 Championship QF National U20 Shield SF BT Scottish National Leagues BT Scottish Cup QF Swalec Welsh Nat Ch/ship
Sat. 10th and Sun. 11th	Aviva English Premiership (13)	Sat. 14th and Sun. 15th	Aviva English Premiership (14)
Thu. 15th to Sun. 18th	European Champions Cup (5) European Challenge Cup (5)	Sun. 15th Fri. 20th and Sat. 21st	SCOTLAND v WALES (15:00) Aviva English Premiership (15) Ulster Bank Irish Leagues
Fri. 16th to Sun. 18th		Fri. 20th to	
Sat. 17th	Greene King IPA Championship BT Scottish Premiership BT Scottish National Leagues Welsh Principality Pr/ship (12) Swalec Welsh Nat Ch/ship Swalec Welsh National Lges Swalec Welsh Plate (4)	Sun. 22nd Sat. 21st	Guinness PRO12 (15) Greene King IPA Championship English National Leagues BT Scottish Premiership BT Scottish National Leagues Swalec Welsh National Lges Swalec Welsh Cup (2)
Thu. 22nd to Sun. 25th	European Champions Cup (6) European Challenge Cup (6)	Fri. 27th and Sat. 28th	Aviva English Premiership (16) Welsh Principality Pr/ship (17)
Sat. 24th	English National Leagues 1, 2 National U20 Ch/ship (3) National U20 Shield QF British & Irish Cup QF BT Scottish Premiership BT Scottish National Leagues Welsh Principality Pr/ship (13) Swalec Welsh Nat Ch/ship Swalec Welsh National Lges Ulster Bank Irish Leagues	Fri. 27th to Sun. 1st Mar. Sat. 28th	Ulster Bank Irish Leagues Guinness PRO12 (16) SCOTLAND v ITALY (14:30) FRANCE v WALES (17:00) RBS U20 Six Nations English National League 3 Swalec Welsh Nat Ch/ship Swalec Welsh National Lges
Fri. 30th and Sat. 31st	Ulster Bank Irish Leagues	**MARCH 2015**	
Fri. 30th to Sun. 1st Feb.	LV= (Anglo-Welsh) Cup (3)	Sun. 1st Fri. 6th and	IRELAND v ENGLAND (15:00)
Sat. 31st	Greene King IPA Championship English National Leagues BT Scottish National Leagues Welsh Principality Pr/ship (14) Swalec Welsh Nat Ch/ship Swalec Welsh National Lges	Sat. 7th Fri. 6th to Sun. 8th Sat. 7th	Ulster Bank Irish Lges 1A, 2A Greene King IPA Championship Guinness PRO12 (17) English National Leagues BT Scottish National Leagues BT Scottish Cup SF Welsh Principality Pr/ship (18) Swalec Welsh Nat Ch/ship Swalec Welsh National Lges
FEBRUARY 2015			
Fri. 6th Fri. 6th to	WALES v ENGLAND (20:05)	Sat. 7th and Sun. 8th	Aviva English Premiership (17)
Sun. 8th Sat. 7th	LV= (Anglo-Welsh) Cup (4) ITALY v IRELAND (15:30) FRANCE v SCOTLAND (17:00) RBS U20 Six Nations Greene King IPA Championship English National Leagues Welsh Principality Pr/ship (15) Swalec Welsh Nat Ch/ship	Fri. 13th to Sun. 15th Sat. 14th	*LV= (Anglo-Welsh) Cup SF *British & Irish Cup SF WALES v IRELAND (14:30) ENGLAND v SCOTLAND (17:00) RBS U20 Six Nations

English National Leagues 1, 2
National U20 Championship SF
National U20 Shield Final
British & Irish Cup SF
BT Scottish Premiership
BT Scottish National Leagues
Sun. 15th ITALY v FRANCE (15:00)
Fri. 20th and
Sat. 21st Greene King IPA Championship
Sat. 21st ITALY v WALES (12:30)
SCOTLAND v IRELAND (14:30)
ENGLAND v FRANCE (17:00)
RBS U20 Six Nations
English National League 3
Welsh Principality Pr/ship (19)
Sun. 22nd LV= (Anglo-Welsh) Cup Final
*BUCS Finals (Twickenham)
Fri. 27th to
Sun. 29th Greene King IPA Championship
Guinness PRO12 (18)
Sat. 28th English National Leagues
BT Scottish National Leagues
Swalec Welsh Nat Ch/ship
Swalec Welsh National Lges
Swalec Welsh Cup QF
Swalec Welsh Plate QF
Ulster Bank Irish Lges 1A, 2A
Sat. 28th and
Sun. 29th Aviva English Premiership (18)

APRIL 2015
Sat. 4th British & Irish Cup Final
Welsh Principality Pr/ship (20)
Swalec Welsh Nat Ch/ship
Swalec Welsh National Lges
Fri. 10th to
Sun. 12th Guinness PRO12 (19)
Sat. 11th Greene King IPA Championship
English National Leagues
Swalec Welsh Nat Ch/ship
Swalec Welsh National Lges
Swalec Welsh Cup SF
Ulster Bank Irish Lges 1A, 2A
Sat. 11th and
Sun. 12th Aviva English Premiership (19)
Fri. 17th to
Sun. 19th *European Champions Cup SF
*European Challenge Cup SF
Greene King IPA Championship
English National Leagues
Sat. 18th BT Scottish Cup Final
Welsh Principality Pr/ship (21)
Swalec Welsh Nat Ch/ship
Swalec Welsh National Lges
Swalec Welsh Plate SF
Fri. 24th to
Sun. 26th Guinness PRO12 (20)
Sat. 25th Aviva English Premiership (20)
Greene King IPA Championship
English National Leagues 1, 2
English Nat Lge 3/Div Play-offs
Welsh Principality Pr/ship (22)

Swalec Welsh Nat Ch/ship
Ulster Bank Irish League 1A SF

MAY 2015
Fri. 1st European Challenge Cup Final
Sat. 2nd European Champions Cup Final
Greene King IPA Ch/ship SF (1)
English National Lge 2 Play-off
English County Ch/ship Shield (1)
Swalec Welsh Cup Final
Swalec Welsh Plate Final
Sun. 3rd National U20 Ch/ship Final
RFU Intermediate Cup Final
RFU Senior Vase Final
RFU Junior Vase Final
Fri. 8th to
Sun. 10th Guinness PRO12 (21)
Sat. 9th Greene King IPA Ch/ship SF (2)
English County Ch/ship (1)
Welsh Principality Pr/ship SF
Army v Navy (Babcock Trophy)
Ulster Bank Irish Lge 1A Final
Sat. 9th and
Sun. 10th Aviva English Premiership (21)
HSBC 7s World Series
(Glasgow)
Fri. 15th to
Sun. 17th Guinness PRO12 (22)
Sat. 16th English County Ch/ship (2)
Welsh Principality Pr/ship Final
Sat. 16th and
Sun. 17th Aviva English Premiership (22)
HSBC 7s World Series
(Twickenham)
Fri. 22nd to
Sun. 24th *Aviva English Premiership SF
*Guinness PRO12 SF
Sat. 23rd Greene King IPA Ch/ship Final (1)
English County Ch/ship (3)
Sat. 30th Aviva English Premiership Final
Greene King IPA Ch/ship Final (2)
Guinness PRO12 Final
Sun. 31st England v Barbarians
English County Ch/ship Final
(Bill Beaumont Cup)
English Cty Ch/ship Div 2 Plate
Final
English Cty Ch/ship Shield Final

Key
TRC = The Rugby Championship, successor
competition to the Tri-Nations
* indicates dates and times to be confirmed